Allum - Graves.

BODY BROKEN
BODY BLESSED

Another book by Sue Mosteller

My Brother, My Sister (1972)

Books by Jean Vanier about L'Arche communities

The Heart of L'Arche (1995)
An Ark for the Poor (1995)
Network of Friends (2 volumes) (1992, 1994)
From Brokenness to Community (1992)
Community and Growth (1989)

Sue Mosteller, C.S.J.

BODY BROKEN
BODY BLESSED

Reflections from Life in Community

NOVALIS / E.J. DWYER

Photos: L'Arche Daybreak

Cover Photo: Gord Henry and Joe Child from the L'Arche Daybreak
    Community in Richmond Hill, Ontario

Illustrations: Zizi Pascal

First published in Canada, 1996, by Novalis. First published in Australia,
New Zealand and the Pacific Islands, 1996, by E. J. Dwyer (Australia) Pty.
Ltd.

© 1996 Novalis

Novalis, 49 Front Street, East, 2nd Floor,
Toronto, Ontario, Canada, M5E 1B3

E. J. Dwyer (Australia) Pty. Ltd., Unit 13, Perry Park
33 Maddox Street, Alexandria NSW 2015, Australia

Canadian Cataloguing-in-Publication Data

Mosteller, Sue, 1933-
    Body broken, body blessed: reflections from life in
community

(L'Arche collection)

ISBN 2-89088-785-5

    1. Arche Daybreak (Association). 2. Church work
with the mentally handicapped--Ontario--Richmond
Hill--Catholic Church. 3. Church work with the
developmentally disabled--Ontario--Richmond Hill--
Catholic Church. 4. Group homes for the mentally
handicapped--Ontario--Richmond Hill. I. Title.
II. Series.

BX2347.8.M4M68 1996   267'.182   C96-900327-7

National Library of Australia Cataloguing-in-Publication Data

Mosteller, Sue, 1933-
    Body broken, body blessed

    ISBN 0 85574 390 5.

    1. Handicapped – Biography. I. Title

    362.40922

Printed and bound in Canada.

CONTENTS

PREFACE

L'Arche was founded to offer a home to people who, because of an intellectual disability, were wounded and unable to find it or manage it for themselves. In the communities of L'Arche, and in my home community of L'Arche Daybreak near Toronto, core members (people with disabilities) and assistants (those who come to help) live together in common and share their lives in a household, forming one body. We have been surprised to discover that the body, broken by human weakness and blessed by many diverse gifts, offers more than a home, and to more people than the disabled.

Assistants as well as core members come to L'Arche wounded by circumstances, accidents, structures, rejection, abuse, weakness, stupidity, bad choices, and losses. It all takes so much time, and it is only now, after thirty years, that we reflect with wonder on the ways in which so many of us, members of our communities, are standing up, claiming our lives, integrating our losses, and assuming our true identity as men and women of peace.

Besides being a home, L'Arche has been a place where core members have matured beyond all our expectations. Bonds of friendship have held us in a safe network where we have worked through and integrated some of the personal losses, rejection, and pains of the past and of the present. This form of growth and maturation takes quite a long time, but it is more and more evident that the majority of core members in L'Arche have made interior passages of some magnitude, so that they now claim their lives and their dignity. By doing so, they are telling us that they are not simply people who are needy, but they are also people of courage, gift, and interiority. Many core members have not only been supported to claim something for themselves, but they have also offered support for assistants and others to do likewise. We were not so aware of this when we began to create homes together thirty years ago, but we are astonished today as we witness people's growth and inner transformation shining like a light in a very dark world.

In this book I seek to share some of the wonder of living faithful relationships over a period of time, in the broken and blessed body of a community. This book is given with the hope that all who seek to live a full and fruitful life beyond their wounds and their fears will recognize family life and community as the place to do that. It is given with the hope that all of us who support each other in creating *home*, whether in the family, the parish, or the intentional community, may be inspired to realize that, alone we are poor, but together we are rich in the potential for fabulous growth and transformation – right in the heart of our struggle to live together as men and women of peace.

Janice and Michael

INTRODUCTION

In our emotional and psychological adolescence and naiveté, we complain: the family is dysfunctional, education is useless, jobs are all taken, homelessness is on the rise, crime and poverty are rampant, organized religion has failed, there is corruption in politics, and the older generation has made a mess of the world. In our idealism, we believe that we can change all that, bypass corruption, mobilize, and create a new and better world. We move out into the fray with high hopes and energy, criticizing our parents, blaming the government and organized religion, marching for justice, protesting for equal rights, and working to turn the tide, until we realize how different and difficult we are together as people, how broken is the body of humanity, and how impossible it is to make even the slightest change. Disillusionment sets in and we gradually settle into a world of individuality and complacency, where we are no less naive or complaining. The fact is, we have failed to appreciate and accept the mystery, the blessedness, and the power of community as a place of maturation, change, and transformation.

Caring human relationships are central in our quest to improve conditions, transform hearts, or change the world. Whether we are a body of two in an intimate partnership, or a few more in a nuclear family, or whether we belong to a church group, a twelve-step program, a therapy group, a political party, or an intentional community, we know that life together is at the same time marvelous and terrible, broken and blessed.

Relational life begins at conception, when we actually take up residence in our mother's body and depend entirely upon her life, until that body becomes too confining and we have to move on. After birth, ideally, we find a place in the family body, sharing life and growing through infancy, childhood and adolescence into maturity. This growth happens best when we are together in caring relationships over a long period of time. Then this body becomes too confining and again we move on to create a new one with others or with a partner.

It is mysterious how the blessed body of family or community, which so powerfully binds us together for growth, maturation, and independence, is at the same time the broken body that permanently wounds us, breaking our hearts and our capacity for fulfillment. If we are to change for the better, or if we are to change the world, there is a certain coming-to-terms with this mysterious contradiction!

In truth, I really detest community life! I've lived in community since I was born over sixty years ago, and I experience it as a place of suffering. My siblings say that I, as the youngest of five children, was spoiled, but my experience in that respect was the opposite! It was a place where my brother and sisters seemed to be ahead of me in experience and confidence, because their lives seemed to me to be full and exciting, while mine felt dowdy and lonely. Each member of my family is unique, wonderful and beautiful, but family life was for me the place where my restless heart was also wounded. My parents and siblings were unable to offer the unconditional love that was needed for my growth to wholeness.

At nineteen, in the fifties and before Vatican II, when I went to the convent to become a nun, I was introduced to conformity and discipline for the building of a community of love. Religious community is a place of surrender, where the vows bind me to live with compassion and to love generously. Because the Sisters are my friends and are fabulous, dedicated women, I have grown in gentleness and unselfishness, but the convent has also been the place where my heart yearned for much more human love and affection than was present in that particular body of women religious. Oooff!

L'Arche, an intentional community where men and women with intellectual disabilities, and those who come to assist them, create home together, looked ideal to me when I was thirty-nine years old. It was a body of people with the Poor at the heart of it. It was an international and ecumenical body of friends! But I have to confess that L'Arche is anything but an ideal place for my little heart and spirit! Living together in community with men, women, Anglican, Jewish, Roman Catholic, Muslim, non-believers, hippies, yuppies, Irish, Italian, Brazilian, Dutch, French, English, Tonganese, Australian, gay, straight, married, single, young, older, those with intellectual disabilities and those with emotional and psychological disabilities, is, needless to say, a real challenge for me! Like every other human family, L'Arche is great, but it is also the place where our human differences and limitations, more often than not, make life difficult.

Community is the place that pinches me and limits my individuality. It pushes me much farther than I want to go in my idealism towards loving others, giving myself in a life of service, and trying to change the world. Being faithful in a body of friends drags me into the experience of their poverty, selfishness, brokenness and darkness, and it forces me into the truth of my own limitations, vulnerabilities, and hardness of heart. That is why I hate community!

When I declare at the very same time that I also love living together with others in family and community, you may think that I am inconsistent! I can live with that - now, because community life, over all these many years, is giving me a stronger sense of my true identity. Despite what you might think, I am comfortable living with these contradictory feelings.

Family and community is what home is all about. The network of relationships offers me a place to live, to grow and to mature. In this milieu there is a wonderful mutuality where I not only receive support and comfort from others, but I also have a channel for my gifts of care and love for others. When I am strong in the family, I am fulfilled by giving affirmation and love to others who may be suffering, and when I am fragile, there is a network of people, committed to me, who catch me and hold me on the way through disillusionment and anger to integration and new beginnings.

Community life is a beautiful garden, a place of growth, where I am bonded with other people to share and support the growth and the fecundity of each one. Even with its limits, community living is "good ground" where, rooted, I can grow in stature and a sense of who I am in relationship to authority figures, peers, and weaker members. Community is the place where maternity, paternity, and childlikeness flower in each of us to enrich, sustain, temper,

and call forth the beauty and the fragrance of each precious life.

Community life is a place where illusions and deceptions about myself and others are stripped away, and where I touch the true metal of my deepest aspirations and of my freedom. The differences and difficulties that rub me the wrong way frustrate and infuriate me, file away the rough edges of my selfishness and invite me to put my money where my mouth is. For better or for worse, community is the place where I am constantly having *to choose and to live, under these particular circumstances, at this particular moment in time, with this particular person,* to be a woman of peace. It is the place where mysteriously, without fail, my heart will be transformed! It is so awful – but it is also fabulous, wonderful and liberating! I love it and wouldn't change it for the world!

For me, community life is a place of communion with others and with God. It is in community that I discover my need for God's Spirit and grace, for God's unconditional love. My deep, abiding belief in the presence of God in my life and in the life of my family and community is in, through, and under, all that is written in this book.

The stories of Lloyd, Loretta, Bill, and others that follow are some of the "success" stories of people who came to find a home in our communities and who found something more. The stories witness to the fact that community is a difficult and wonderful place, a broken and blessed place, a place that is full of holes and full of grace. Although the stories happened in L'Arche, they have a universal quality and could have been lived in any community or family body where people are trying to be faithful to each other in love and commitment.

This book is written with the hope that we will be inspired by David, Carol, Tracy, and the others who found L'Arche and who made L'Arche a place of healing and growth. Relationships change us and change the world. Friendship, marriage, partnership, intimacy, and community life are wonderful places of formation and healing; they are difficult, wounding, comforting and demanding places of compassion and liberation. Lived faithfully over time and according to Gospel values, community life transforms us unimaginably. Rosie, Peter, Bill, myself and other unlikely teachers whose stories are here, have grown against enormous odds, testifying by their lives to the power of this truth.

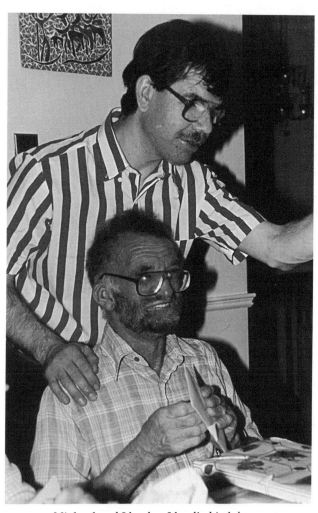

Michael and Lloyd at Lloyd's birthday party

I

A PLACE TO FIND HOME

Our first home, the womb, is a place of growth, protection and nourishment. From there we move and take a place in the family, our second home. Family, too, can be a good, safe and nurturing ground for growth in the face of new challenges. Later, we move again and have the opportunity to create home, possibly with a partner, for ourselves and for others.

We have images of homeless people: on our streets begging and sleeping in doorways, and on the TV, fleeing war, "ethnic cleansing," and famine. They have been torn from their roots, and their faces and their tears touch something deep within us. We do not like what we see and we pass by, or we flick the channel so that we do not have to look, perhaps because these images touch something of our own experience of homelessness. We too have trusted and given ourselves in relationships of friendship and intimacy to others, thinking we were finally home forever, only to be disappointed and heart-broken when the whole thing collapsed and disappeared. We know the painful feeling of being cut off or set adrift from relationships that nourished and protected us.

When we enjoy good and safe relationships, we may take them for granted, but we suffer when they are broken or gone. The pain of homelessness kills our spirits. It breaks something inside and takes away our capacity to trust and our will to live. The passage through grief and broken trust to new hope and renewed trust is seldom made alone, and it takes a very long time. It is not easy, but it is possible.

Lloyd claims a second family

His home was his castle. For fifty years Lloyd lived with his parents and laboured on the land with his father, raising cattle and the food to feed them. His parents and sisters, his dog, his cows, his daily routine supported him so that he could live a very "normal" life, even if he was slow intellectually. He was a worker and he loved his work. His life and his work gave him a sense of dignity, especially when his father changed the "Kerman Farm" sign on the barn to read "Kerman and Son."

Lloyd loved his family and was close to each of his sisters. Their friends were his friends and he was well-loved in the neighbouring farm community. When his sister Erma married and left the farm he went with his mother to visit her in Vancouver. He knew little but life on the family farm for his first fifty years. His parents cared for him, and as they aged the tables turned and Lloyd became their faithful caregiver.

Things began to change when Lloyd lost first his father and constant companion on the job. Without his father there was no job, because Lloyd was unable to carry the farm alone. He was devastated.

Not too long after that, he lost his mother and confidant. She had been the steady, loving, welcoming and accepting presence for his entire life. In her absence he felt abandoned.

When he came to live at Daybreak, he was in a state of shock. From the intimacy of the home and family, he was plunged into a large group of strangers. Even with the support of his sisters, he suffered enormously and he said more than once that he wished he could die. He walked around in what seemed to be a trance for nearly five years, able to communicate yes or no, but not much else. He was employed on the Daybreak farm, but his father was absent, the Daybreak farm workers were unskilled, and the Holsteins that he cherished were absent. He disliked the herd of Jerseys. In his heart, he was homeless.

Lloyd was silent, uncomplaining, and cooperative. For many years he lived very quietly, carrying his pain deep within. We did not know the exact suffering he endured, but it was obvious that he was deeply, deeply anguished. A few times he was hospitalized because of depression.

It is difficult to say what happened, except that after a very long time Lloyd began to enjoy a friendship with Michael, another man in his home. Michael was slow to speak and needed quite a bit of support because of seizures. Lloyd and Michael spent more and more time together, sometimes silently, but often in conversation. Lloyd had time to listen and Michael had lots to say. Lloyd began to help Michael with dressing and toileting. On Michael's birthday, Lloyd made a speech and said, "Michael is a good man and a good friend!"

Unobtrusively, one of the assistants, Phil, became very good friends with Lloyd and they often went out for a beer or to hockey games together. Phil was even able to tease Lloyd about Holsteins and get away with it! Then Steve, another friend, made some trips with Lloyd, and Lloyd, more and more able to speak, talked about Steve as his friend, too.

Lloyd regularly visited his sister Ruth in Oshawa. Whenever they were together they walked down to the original farm property which has since become a cemetary. One day Lloyd expressed a desire to visit his sister Elsie in Florida. It was arranged, and thus began a series of visits, several years in a row. With a twinkle in his eye, he took the teasing about flying off on his winter vacations by retorting, "Phil, you should go away on a vacation, to give *us* a break!"

Lloyd quietly assumed responsibility in his home. He cooked, supported his housemates, said a few words of welcome to new assistants, and expanded his after-dinner prayer from "mom and dad" to a longer list of family and friends.

Keith, an assistant, and Lloyd were good friends and spent quality time together when Keith helped Lloyd with his bath. Lloyd knew of Keith's relationship with another assistant, Jeffi. As they talked about it, Keith told Lloyd that he thought he wanted to ask Jeffi to marry him. Lloyd encouraged him. Together, the two of them planned the proposal which included going together to get rings made from a family heirloom. When Keith and Lloyd went together to pick up the rings on the day he was to propose to Jeffi, they weren't ready. Keith was despondent. Walking home, he told Lloyd that he was worried because the "conditions" would never be the same again. Lloyd, putting his hand on Keith's back in support, walked along for quite a long time, then patted him and said, "It is good, Keith. Don't worry. It is good." That word, uttered with such conviction and love, went straight to Keith's heart and renewed his flagging spirit.

Lloyd chose to become a member of the Richmond Hill United Church and proved to be a faithful one! He joined the men's group and helped build the church float for the annual "fair day" parade, and then he showed up to ride on the float in the parade.

People were taken off guard when Lloyd wanted to audition for a part in Daybreak's 25th Anniversary Gala production, *One Heart at a Time*. He was given one line about Holstein cows, and he excitedly told people, "Guess what? I'm going to be in the Gala!" Unfortunately Lloyd fell sick and was unable to perform or attend the February gala.

Later that year, in May, Lloyd was still not feeling well because of a weak heart, but his housemates went ahead with plans to celebrate his birthday a week early because the actual day fell during a holiday weekend.

His sisters and three of his close friends were invited for his favourite chicken dinner. On Sunday afternoon the guests entered the barn-like atmosphere of his home where black-and-white streamers, black-and-white table napkins, and a black-and-white tablecloth set the "Holstein" theme. Lloyd was constantly teased for his love of everything Holstein.

Before going to the dinner table, guests and housemates sat with Lloyd in the living room around a lighted candle. Mary played a song on the guitar and then each person spoke to Lloyd. Larry said he was grateful that Lloyd had welcomed him into the home for the summer and had taught him some of the routines. Jean-Baptiste, having come from France only a year before, thanked Lloyd for being so patient with him while he was learning English. Linda, a house mate, told him that she loved to live with him because he was such a "good man," and Dorothy, his sister, cried and thanked him for being the best possible brother! After two or three had spoken, Mary quietly played and sang the refrain, "Laudate Domino": (Let us praise the Lord!), and then the next person had a chance to speak to Lloyd. Martha remarked that Lloyd had made her conscious of cows and that now she could never pass a cow without thinking of Holsteins and of Lloyd. Keith, now married to Jeffi, thanked him for his encouragement to propose to Jeffi. Phil, now an ordained minister, began by teasing Lloyd about his poor choice of a hockey team that did so poorly in the play-offs, and then he thanked Lloyd for drawing the images for, and helping to make the beautiful stole for his April ordination celebration. He thanked Lloyd for investing him with the stole during his ordination ceremony.

Finally, Lloyd had the chance to speak about himself and his hopes and dreams. Very quietly he said that he was excited because in February, when Daybreak put on its 25th Anniversary Gala, he was sick and unable to be in it, but now, in two weeks' time, he was going to make a joke about Holsteins in the play, *One Heart at a Time*, at the theatre! He thanked everyone for their gifts and for coming to his party.

After a delicious dinner, other friends and acquaintances dropped in for cake and ice cream. Just as people were finishing, a humungous Holstein cow came prancing up the stairs from the basement! The music was perfect as the two people, dressed in a rented Holstein suit, romped, danced, "licked" Lloyd's face, stepped on his feet, patted his head, and finally plopped down in his lap!

As the cow disappeared, Martha brought the cards and gifts and sat beside Lloyd, offering him one gift at a time. People sat around him as he opened each one, and she helped him to read the writing on the cards, to recognize the person who had given a gift, to put the wrappings aside, and to pass the gift so each person could look at it.

Finally, Jean-Baptiste lit the candle and Mary took the guitar once more to lead us in prayer. For fifteen minutes, people had the opportunity to pray spontaneously and give thanks for Lloyd and for the gift of his life. Lloyd also prayed in thanksgiving for family and friends who came to his birthday.

On the Tuesday following his birthday celebration, Lloyd was hospitalized with an intestinal obstruction. On Thursday he suffered heart failure and, surrounded by those who had so beautifully celebrated his life, he died. One week after his funeral, the performance of *One Heart at a Time* was dedicated to Lloyd's memory by the members of his grieving community.

It took a long time, and we aren't even sure how it happened, but Lloyd had very gradually come to terms with his enormous loss of home. Somewhere, somehow, he overcame his overwhelming desire to die and made a choice to live! He risked. He stood up again and took an important place in his home and in the hearts of his friends. And by his choice to be home, by his gentle, quiet, fun-loving presence, his life became a gift for others.

Our challenge to claim and reclaim *home*

When we know the pain of abandonment, loss or rejection, there is hope for us as well. Like Lloyd, we need patience and a deep respect for the time it takes to grieve our real losses and to own them as our own. We need lots of time and support to give up our expectation that someone can erase or change what actually happened that wounded us. We need to share and ask for support in our network of friends, of family, church, or community where people will not be scandalized when they hear that our once cherished relationships are complicated, difficult, less than perfect, or gone altogether. And gradually, when the time is right, we need encouragment to step through and beyond our grief into new and renewed relationships of trust, where we once again recover our ability to care for others and our sense of humour. Lloyd's example points the way!

Loretta and Jessamyn

II

A PLACE TO HOLD MY SHAKY HEART

A theme of novels and biographies, a central topic of songs and poetry, and a main subject in the theatre, is the universal experience of the broken heart. Each of us longs to live, vicariously or really, a unique relationship of unconditional love and trust that brings us fulfillment, safety, stability, and joy. Our hearts are tuned and our lives are geared to look for the one person who will answer this primal cry of the human spirit.

Our needy hearts are easily seduced and deceived. When we sense the mutuality of attraction, our hearts are taken and we blindly invest ourselves too much and too soon. Then, when darkness begins to colour the relationship, it is too late to prevent the deep pain of disillusionment, hurt and loss. We speak of the experience by saying, "My heart is broken."

Mending the broken heart takes one on a very long road through hurt, anger, fear, resentment and the experience of existential loneliness. It demands a conscious choice to give up the hope and expectation of unconditional love by accepting that it is simply not possible. It means allowing space and freedom to love and be loved with less-than-perfect love. For some, healing means recognizing and accepting that unconditional love begins and ends with the author of love, God, who tells us in Scripture, "I have loved you with an everlasting love and you are mine."

No medicine touches the pain of a broken heart. No reason embraces the experience. The heart accepts no substitute for a unique relationship of love. It may be deceived, seduced, and disappointed, but it continues to dream and to hope that love is possible.

Loretta engages her broken heart

Loretta is a typical young adult, who loves partying, dancing, music, and TV. She enjoys shopping for new outfits. Holidays are important for her and she likes to go to new and faraway places, as well as to visit old friends. She likes her birthday, when she is special and can choose the people who will come to her party, as well as the party site, which is usually an upbeat restaurant. Loretta loves a drink and needs some help to know when to stop. She likes to be invited out and to have plans for the weekends.

Loretta has an incredibly loving heart. She is attached to the people of her household and she can be with each one in a unique way. She says, "I love little Carol," and she does. Carol smiles when she sees Loretta and they embrace for a long moment, before Loretta begins to dance and Carol follows along. Loretta was the first to prompt Carol, who doesn't speak, to sing words to "Happy Birthday." Loretta is wonderful with Peter. She loves him like a brother and encourages him when he is feeling sad. When he becomes anxious and starts to bite his hand, Loretta talks him through it, not leaving him until he feels more secure. She is sometimes the only one with whom Janice, fighting chronic depression, will relate. Loretta simply stays in there with her until she gets an answer or a hug. Jan trusts her because Loretta understands, and loves her freely, with trust and compassion.

At an early age Loretta was separated from family and she suffered enormously from the lack of consistently loving relationships. Her broken history includes being placed in a large facility for the disabled when she was very young, followed by placement in a series of seven foster homes. In each case she was initially welcomed, she invested her affection in the people who welcomed her, and she eventually lost, because when her affective needs became too much for her hosts, Loretta was up for a new placement. Her heart, so yearning to love and be loved, was broken many, many times.

Her need for one "special" relationship was an obsession by the time she came to Daybreak in her mid-twenties. Living together with assistants who were open to friendship was perfect, so Loretta began to focus first on Kathy, one of the assistants, hoping to become unique for her, and hoping to capture all of Kathy's attention. She teased her, insisted that Kathy accompany her wherever she went, sat next to her at the table and spoke of her constantly when Kathy was absent. She put little gifts in Kathy's room, followed her about the house and clung to her during community gatherings and worship services.

Initially, Kathy may have been flattered to receive so much affection from Loretta, but gradually it became too demanding and she began to withdraw. Loretta tried desperately to regain the affection that she knew she was losing, and finally became desperate. She showed her anger by being mean and even violent. For no reason, she would suddenly start yelling profanities or throwing objects at Kathy. After it was all over, Loretta would point to her heart and cry out, "It hurts! It hurts too much!" Later she would apologize and promise to do better, but of course she could not do better because her heart was broken. In time, Kathy moved to another home and Loretta, with the help of another assistant, called and/or visited once a week.

For almost a year, Loretta grieved the loss of Kathy's exclusive affection.

The following year she began to become infatuated with Maggie. We were slow, not realizing what was happening until the very same pattern repeated itself. When Maggie withdrew, Loretta again showed the other side of her personality, becoming ugly and violent. When Maggie left that summer to go back to school, Loretta grieved for many months. So many times, in tears, she told us, "It hurts. It hurts too much in my heart!"

The following year when Loretta began to focus on Anne Marie, we began immediately to try to help her to make this one a healthy relationship. We reminded her when she spoke so often of Anne Marie. We set up meetings with the two of them, hoping to "hold" Loretta in the reality of the limits of Anne Marie's friendship. Our talking was quite useless, however, because Loretta's heart was given to Anne Marie. When it became necessary to limit the meetings, Loretta's irrational behaviours returned. One day, not knowing anything about driving, she took the keys to the car and drove the station wagon into the front of the house, displacing the porch and causing the beams to fall and the roof to collapse. Loretta's screams, violence and depression only mirrored her pain. It hurt her – too much! And our reasoning did not touch that pain.

We were getting the message! Loretta could not live the pain of separation and she could not find the communion to satisfy her broken heart.

Loretta had always enjoyed the affection of several community members who knew her as a beautiful and sensitive person, and who stayed close to her in all her ups and downs. It became important to mobilize these less intense but more stable relationships to hold her through some of the times of intense suffering. Susan, the head of her home, devised ways that Loretta would feel "held" by her special, long-term friends. Every Monday, Loretta would plan the week on her calendar with Susan, making time for a dinner out with one of us, a coffee after work, a phone call, or a guest for supper on her cook-night. Trust would build for a time, and then she would, by her actions and by her words, tell us that she was "feeling shaky inside," which meant that she was feeling the loss of uniqueness and special intimacy. When we tried to support and challenge her, she mostly cried, but occasionally she ran away and acted out her feelings. Her friends in the community stood together around her and did not go away. We gave her time; we talked and listened, and we tried to support her with love and with truth. We spelled each other off, and sometimes had to remind each other of the difference between the behaviour – which we could reject – and the person, to whom we were committed.

Her friends accompanied Loretta, one-on-one, to community gatherings where she was likely to meet someone with whom she was having a love-hate relationship; they stayed with her, circulating so that she could meet some people and avoid too much contact with her friend/enemy. Then, if things became unmanageable for her, we would leave with her and do something else together. Occasionally, in a very anxious time, she was too fast for us and managed to throw her juice glass or whack the face of the person with whom she was having difficulty! Our regular, weekly, one-on-one meetings continued for more than three years. We invited her for overnights and we tried to be consistent in our relationships with her. In general, these consistent friendships seemed to help her to have a good time without always searching for the one relationship which would eventually wound her. Over eight years, things slowly started to change.

Some of the relationships that have followed that with Anne Marie have been intense, and Loretta continues to invest herself too much and inappropriately with one particular person. She still suffers each time she realizes, once again, that the other person she particularly loves has a life apart from hers and will never love her unconditionally. Still, she is now more conscious of her pattern, and she is more able to talk about it and to avoid giving herself too much and too fast and then having such long periods of grieving. We who are her friends still do things with her, but her circle is much wider now and her social life more spontaneous. Her episodes today are fewer and much farther between.

Recently Loretta chose to move out of a house where her best friend lived, to a home in the city that would allow her more scope for her social life. It is so amazing to witness her courage, and to watch her become such a beautiful and self-possessed young woman.

Loretta is not cured of her need for a unique relationship of intimacy: she will probably always need support in the realm of friendship because, alone, she tends to go over the edge. Living in a community, though, where several friends are committed to support her when "it hurts too much," has opened the door to many relationships of true mutuality. From this experience she herself has become one of the committed friends around little Carol, Peter and Jan. Loretta needs this mutuality where she is "held" in relationships of friendship and where she, in turn, "holds" others with her beautiful gift of friendship and care.

Our choice to care for one another and ourselves

"Our hearts are restless, O Lord, until they find their rest in Thee," remarked the paramour and saint, Augustine, in the fourth century. The need for unconditional love is written into our flesh, and there is no substitute. As we search for unconditional love in our relationships, we are continually disappointed and disillusioned.

Like Loretta, we need a body of friends where gentleness, compassion and truth surround us on our life-journey, on our heart-journey. That is why it is important to build and belong to a wider family, a community, where we mutually hold onto each other with consistent, though imperfect relationships. Isn't that the gift of twelve-step programs, therapy groups, and prayer groups? "Our hearts are restless, O Lord!" Help us to give and receive support in relationships of true friendship which reflect the unconditional affection that flows from your God-Heart of Love.

Rosie

III

A PLACE
TO BECOME MYSELF

As children, we do not recognize our identity by looking in a mirror, but we see ourselves as others in our family circle see us. As adults in the context of other intimate relationships, we have the opportunity to reject the old and to claim or reclaim a truer identity, a truer sense of ourselves. In consistent, faithful relationships we can choose to reject the voices that tell us we are unworthy and incapable, and gradually we can choose, in freedom, the truth of our beauty and value.

That is why we so desperately need a network of caring relationships in which to live and grow up in the truth. Our hearts are sensitive to the positive and negative messages that we read in the looks and words of friends and relatives. "Will I be loved if I do not measure up? Am I still OK if I fail my exams? Will they throw me away if I say No to some of their expectations of me? Will they respect me even when my behaviour is less than ideal? Will they hold onto me through a tough time, when I have little to give and much to gain from our mutual relationship?" With time and fidelity we come to know the underlying truth of our worth and value. When we claim it and live from it, we are finally free!

Rosie claims her truth

In a condemned nursing home about to close, Debby from Daybreak met Rosie more than ten years ago. Rosie was a tiny, twenty-one-year-old homeless waif, living in a small crib with a grated top, that looked like a cage. It was totally ludicrous to secure the crib's lid, since Rosie could neither sit up by herself, stand or walk. She weighed only forty-three pounds, mainly because her narrowed esophagus prevented her from eating anything as thick as a milkshake. Rosie had no speech, but that didn't really matter either, because her autism apparently separated her from anyone wishing to be close to her. She suffered, too, from a curvature of the spine and she had a hiatus hernia. Besides the physical difficulties, she gave no signs at all of wanting to live and no interest in anything, least of all in people.

Handicapped and abandoned at birth, Rosie suffered a total lack of family and had not one, life-long, consistent relationship, not one experience of being unique and beautiful for another. She had no expression on her face. There was little life in her small body. Lifting her was like lifting a sack of flour. As a young adult, she seemed to have no sense of her identity as a person of value.

Debby told Rosie that for the past two years we had been planning and preparing to welcome some people with physical, as well as intellectual disabilities. She talked about the new home that had been renovated in preparation, and of the team that had gone for special training and was ready to welcome her. Debby asked Rosie if she would like to come and live with us. Never making eye contact, Rosie squirmed to the other side of the crib to get farther away and turned her back on Debby.

When the nursing home closed a few months later, Rosie was placed at Daybreak. After a long preparation, members of the community were excited to welcome her and to offer her a home. So much attention had gone into the planning of this ideal project that we imagined Rosie would feel she had "hit the jackpot" by coming to live with us! At Daybreak we wanted to offer her a beautiful home, her own room, special clothes, medical care, long walks, a program during the day, lots of time for meals, more consistent friendships, and a community of celebration and forgiveness.

Rosie was not interested in any of it and, besides, she had to live a deep bereavement, leaving behind the safety of the only life she had ever known. She stayed very aloof. She cried, and her cries became screams which pierced our ears and lasted for hours on end. She refused to eat, spitting back everything that was put into her mouth. She rocked, banging herself against the wall, never smiled, never looked at anyone directly, and continued to scream most days, for more than two years! Sometimes she would simply stop breathing until her lips were blue, and then D.J., the assistant, would gather her into his arms and go off to the hospital to ensure her revival. Rosie lived in some faraway world of anguish.

It was not easy to stay long with Rosie, so we in the community took turns caring for her and telling her by our words and actions that she was precious and that we wanted her to be a participating member of the community. She would have none of it, refusing any return for the love and care being poured out. Our psychiatrist told us that, convinced of her nothingness by such radical abandonment, she was proving how hateful she was. Our task, he told us, was to believe more in her beauty than she believed in her hatefulness! Rosie's conviction was like steel. We needed one another and friends to hold on in front of her.

It was two or three years before we noticed the first signs that Rosie was really *in there*! She became comfortable with John, one of the other core members in her household who loved her from the beginning and who showered her with his attention. She could accept his kisses and his affection, and once in awhile, she even smiled. Then, she allowed

D.J., the head of the home, and Mary, who was responsible for her Day Program, to hold her in their arms for a time and to talk with her. She became more relaxed with Zenia, another assistant, splashing in the bath, sitting quietly while her hair was being dried, or making contented noises while she was being dressed. Slowly there were signs of trust: less rocking, sometimes eating without a fuss, smiling, and a glance into the face of the person who was with her. For the care-givers who gave so much and received so little, a glance of recognition from Rosie was a precious gift!

We did not expect to have to believe in Rosie's worth in the face of opposition from the medical profession. The General Hospital refused her because she was too small, and the Children's Hospital refused her because she was too old! Right in front of Rosie the first surgeon asked, "Why would you want to do corrective surgery on *her*?" After the sixth surgeon refused to do the necessary surgery because of her many other limitations, one of our Board Members, a doctor, influenced a colleague to scrape and widen her esophagus, and to correct the hernia. This was a turning point for Rosie.

She was moving about on the second day after surgery and ready to leave the hospital on the third! She began actually to enjoy her food and she devoured bowl after bowl of spaghetti, gained weight, and gained energy. She showed eagerness to feed herself and took delight in snatching food from the plate of the person sitting beside her at the table! She was actually looking into people's eyes when they spoke to her, and she could risk giggling when she was teased. Every day there were new signs that Rosie was *in there*, and was choosing to express herself and choosing to live.

A few months after her surgery, tipping the scales at sixty pounds, Rosie began to crawl! She loved it because she could get herself to the floor radiators or move out into the sun where the heat gave her pleasure. She laughed too as she skidded away from those trying to catch her.

One day when she was twenty-five years old, Rosie, holding onto the coffee table, rose up into a standing position! In a very short time she learned to take some steps and she toddled about all on her own. To see Rosie walking even unsteadily through the home was like having a tiny glimpse of resurrection. She knew where her room was, and she felt free to leave the crowded dinner table to go off for some time alone. Later, she might toddle back to join the group and enjoy some dessert.

Zenia and Rosie became fast friends! Rosie had no speech, but Zenia, an extrovert, loved to talk and was seldom silent when she and Rosie were together. "Oh Rosie, you are so fabulous!" "You know, Rosie, your hair is gorgeous, so let's use the curling iron today and see what happens." "Rosie, do you know how absolutely beautiful you are? Just look at yourself in the mirror! Come now! Let's go and show everyone how ravishing you look this morning!"

At one point, Zenia planned a trip with Rosie to New York City to visit a former assistant. We thought it was foolish and we told Zenia, "Rosie will scream all the way to New York on the plane." Zenia wasn't worried about that. True, Rosie screamed all the way to the airport at seven a.m., but once they were on the plane she loved it, attracting the attention of the stewardesses and enjoying the refreshments! One of the best moments was the shopping trip to Bloomingdale's, where Rosie bought some new outfits and was later named, on awards night at Daybreak, the best-dressed woman in the community!

Clara lived for eight months as an assistant in the home, daily bathing and helping to feed Rosie without receiving any sign of recognition or affection from her. But on the day when Clara had an altercation with another assistant which upset her, Rosie seemed to know what to do. Bursting into tears, Clara ducked into Rosie's empty room and sat on the bed, crying into her hands. She was completely unaware of Rosie coming in and climbing onto the bed. Suddenly, Rosie plunked herself into Clara's lap, looked directly into her tear-stained face, and began to laugh! It was a deliberate attempt on Rosie's part to console her friend, Clara.

Rosie recently celebrated her tenth anniversary at Daybreak. The house was jammed with over thirty old friends who came to celebrate her. While Rosie allowed people to hug her, looked at them when they spoke to her, killed herself laughing, ate up a storm, and walked about like the queen of the castle, each of us spoke of the marvel of Rosie Decker. Her life has touched us profoundly and we echo the sentiments of Zenia, who testified, "Rosie, you have changed my heart in ways that I could never have imagined, and you are one of the most beautiful and courageous women I have ever known."

Rosie still screams. She knows anguish. But her choice to live is unfaltering, and she tells us by the radiance of her presence that, in her heart-of-hearts, she is changed. She has somewhere chosen to be Rosie, accepted to be Rosie, and believed over and above her many limitations, that she has a place in this world. With her gentle, beautiful and true identity, Rosie has touched the lives of literally hundreds of people.

The truth makes us free

Our broken families have been unable to grace us with a totally positive image of ourselves. The old voices, ringing continually in our ears, tell us that we were never quite good enough and that we didn't quite meet the necessary standards of "wonderful" or "precious". The old "tapes" of memory are powerful demons, robbing us of the truth that our lives, whatever their limits, are of incredible value and worth.

Consistent and caring contact with family members and friends is the place where others believe when we cannot. A family or community offers us a space to grieve, as well as an environment to support others in small ways when they are grieving. Family holds us and calls us. When we are strong we can be there for others, encouraging them in their true value and worth, and when we are weak, we can buy time and safe passage back to health and truth.

Finding and claiming a true identity is a life-work, demanding covenant relationships and a deep respect for time. Slowly, slowly we journey through difficult passages from the lie of our worthlessness into the truth of our beauty and importance. Family is always broken and never perfect so there are many setbacks on the way. Community is always "full of holes," wounding us and unable to meet our total need for affirmation. But in these same blessed bodies of consistent, faithful, covenant relationships, we, like Rosie, learn to trust, to crawl, and one day, to stand up and take a true and significant place in the world.

Bill van Buren, Henri Nouwen, and Sue Mosteller

IV

A PLACE TO ENJOY A HISTORY

Our life history begins in the blessed body of a family. All the ways that we live together, share the space, create rituals for meals, celebrate graduation, experience a tragedy, relate with relatives, vacation together, move, prepare for a marriage, await a new baby, or live through the death of a loved one, are written into our life story. Living together in the family for the first years of life, we take our places and gain a sense of ourselves in relationship to others. With time and a sense of our history, we are readied to move beyond the immediate family and make history with a new and wider body of people. When we get together as family or community, we remember and reconnect with the past that brought us to the present.

Unfortunately every family is dysfunctional, so we are wounded as well as grounded by our history and by our family. The family is a broken body where irreconcilable differences, disillusionment and broken trust damage one's self-image and break inner confidence. Some of us have no experience of a consistent, loving, safe history, and we suffer feelings of inadequacy, self-pity, shame and blame. We feel unprepared to risk forging bonds with others, and thus making history with them.

How amazing it is to discover that our history, fragmented and suffering from the brokenness of family, is most often healed and changed within the same family or another body of caring, committed people. How amazing it is when we begin to feel loved well enough to walk through our pain and to claim our lives from those who wounded us and who continue to have power to destroy us. How wonderful for us and for others when, with time and affection, we gain enough inner freedom and confidence to let the old enemies go, and to recommit ourselves to family and community life with new confidence and hope.

Bill claims a history in the community

Several years ago, Bill, one of the core members at Daybreak, was invited to make a life-story-book with pictures and letters from relatives and friends recounting incidents from his history. He quickly refused. Other people had done it and were thrilled to be in touch with their past, but Bill was clearly not interested. Even a conversation about life-story-books made him angry and rude. His reactions were so strong and persistent that the subject was finally dropped and the project no longer considered for Bill. Those who extended this invitation were unaware of the many good reasons Bill had to decline.

Bill's little mother was a simple woman, unable to cope with six children. His father was a poor man with a drinking problem, erratic and unemployed much of the time. There was certainly emotional and physical abuse in this family. Bill has few memories of home and recounts only two: falling from the back of his father's friend's truck and cracking his head open, and one day being taken without warning from his home by social workers, never to return. Separated from his parents and siblings and placed in a series of foster homes, he remembers with sadness and anger some of the ways he was treated and punished by his foster parents as a small boy. His own family was absent.

A scrawny sixteen-year-old, Bill was the first core member to be welcomed to the community of Daybreak when it opened in 1969. He came from a boarding school for intellectually disabled children, and he lived in Daybreak's first home with the founders, Steve and Ann Newroth and their infant son, Jean Frederick. It was his first experience of "normal" family life, so that at the end of the two months, Bill asked, "Steve and Ann, do you think you could be my parents?"

For fifteen years after coming to Daybreak, Bill had no contact with his family. One day, when he was thirty-one years old, his father telephoned, wanting to reconnect with him. Bill was thrilled and afraid. They were able to spend a little positive time together, after which his dad invited him to come home to live with him. Bill's hopes soared, but at the same time he experienced bad dreams and fits of anxiety. He would angrily tell us that he was leaving to live with his family, and in the next breath he would cry and say that he was afraid because his father was unwell and was threatening him. In a panic, he agreed to go home with his dad, yet immediately afterwards he begged us to let him move farther away from his father to a safer house. His father often left big gaps of time between visits, suddenly reappearing for another span of time, keeping Bill on an emotional roller coaster. During that year Bill had the joy of reconnecting briefly with two of his sisters, only to be deeply and abruptly disappointed when it became clear that his sisters were unable to make him part of their lives. Towards the end of two stormy years during which Bill was badly hurt, confused and frightened, his father called and announced that his mother had died. Bill had not seen her since he was a small child, but this news plunged him into grief. He went with his dad to her funeral but not to the burial. At the time, Bill's father was ailing, but Bill did not realize that. Less than two months later, another call came to say that Bill's father had died. It was almost too much, but Bill chose to go to his funeral. For a very long time he grieved whenever he thought or prayed for his father. With the help of several people in his life who loved him and felt committed to him, Bill gradually worked through some of his mixed emotions and especially his anger and deep sadness.

Jane was responsible for Bill's household and was especially attentive to him during this time. She realized Bill's need for one-on-one time with close friends, beginning with herself. They regularly went to a local spot for coffee and donuts, where Jane had a wonderful, listening ear. Jane also kept Bill's friends informed of his need so they too could support him.

Kay and her family, friends of the community for many years, "adopted" Bill and have been his second family. Kay stepped into the picture when she saw that many of the core members of Daybreak enjoyed going occasionally to their families for weekends, and that Bill had no family. She visited first, having dinner regularly in Bill's home, coming to worship with her husband and children, and taking Bill out to McDonald's for a hamburger. Then she invited him to go to their home, first for dinner, then for weekends, and finally for Christmas. Kay has faithfully supported him and lovingly welcomed him into the heart of their family like a mother for the past twenty years. After his parents' death, Kay took a particular interest in Bill and gave him time, presence and care.

Joe and Stephanie were young, single assistants in Bill's home in the early seventies. They were all about the same age at the time. Stephanie teases Bill with memories of his sharing a room in that house with Ken, and of how Ken's side of the room was so neat and tidy, and Bill's, a disaster zone! Joe reminds Bill of the time Bill bet him that he could keep quiet, not saying one word for ten minutes! Joe won the bet when, after thirty seconds, Bill yelled out, "I can't stand it!" Joe and Stephanie and their four children were especially supportive of Bill following his parents' deaths.

Henri, the pastor of Daybreak, is Bill's very special friend. Henri and Bill travel and spend time together, and when Bill lost his parents, Henri counselled him and helped him to name what was happening to him. Henri gave Bill permission to be angry and to be sad for all that he had lost throughout his childhood, and Bill had ample opportunity, in the safety of Henri's presence, to speak about his losses and to weep.

Last year, at the end of his twenty-fifth year in the community, Bill surprised people when he announced that he wanted to do his life-story-book! He quickly qualified his decision by saying he wanted to do it only if he could begin the story at age sixteen, when he came to Daybreak. He asked his two good friends, Joe and Mary Egan, to help him with the project. They have lived and worked in the community for more than twenty years and were integral to Bill's history. Together they wrote to all the people, former assistants and friends that they remembered from his past twenty-five years, inviting each one to write Bill a letter and send a memory and a picture for his life-story-book. Bill also allowed Mary and Joe to send the same letter to his two closest blood sisters with whom he felt a special bond.

Bill went several times to the Egans' home when the letters and pictures began to come back. Together with their three children, they read Bill's letters aloud. The letters sparked Bill's memory and he interrupted, talked endlessly, and laughed, recounting good times and hard times with those people who were helping him remember the events of his past life. He explained the pictures in great detail, remembering how he felt at the time and what he was saying when the picture was snapped. Unfortunately, his sisters, as well as some other friends important in Bill's history, were unable to grasp the significance of a reply, and so far they have failed to respond. In the process Bill named them and asked why they had not answered, and sometimes cried, expressing feelings of abandonment.

Beginning with pictures of young, skinny Bill in his teens, the life-story-book is full of sacred memories. His friends remind him of the times they were together, of their love for him, and of their respect for the ways that he has integrated his past with his present, and grown in stature.

Dear Bill,

. . .

Another event that really stands out in our relationship together was our trip to Washington. You remember that beautiful ballroom where we were invited to give a talk to about 2,000 people? I was quite nervous because I knew that the people expected a lot. While I delivered the talk, you were at my side turning the pages. At one point, when I said something important to impress the audience, you leaned into the microphone and made that funny remark, "Oh, I've heard that before!" Everyone was impressed all right! I still remember how after the talk, you went around shaking hands with people and how they liked you and said to me, "What a wonderful friend you have!"

. . .

The last years have not been easy for you because of the physical problems with your heart, your walking and your breathing, but I really admire the way you live these struggles. . . . You are a man with many sorrows and many joys, a man who cries a lot and who laughs a lot, and sometimes your tears and your smile are there together.

. . .

Now we are both becoming a little older and we both feel it. That is why you keep saying, "If I die first, Henri will be upset, and if Henri dies first, I will be upset. Maybe we should die together."

. . .

I love to travel with you, Bill, and I am proud that you are my friend.

> With love,
> Henri Nouwen

Dear Bill,

. . .

I think one of the most privileged moments together was going to your father's funeral. He had visited you less than a week before he died, although he was obviously very sick. I remember that after he died, and as we talked about him together, you realized that your father must have loved you to have made the effort to come and see you. I think that allowed you to forgive him for the times that had been difficult in your relationship with him. It seems you were able to let go of your feelings and realize that life had not been easy for your father either. All this shows me what a tender, loving heart you have . . .

Love,
Jane Powell

Dear Bill,

. . .

Remember when we went with Henri to give talks in North Carolina? The first night you began to talk to four hundred people and to tell them of your life at Daybreak. As soon as you mentioned Adam and Rosie, you burst into tears, saying, "I love Adam and he cannot walk. Neither can Rosie." Henri put his arm around you and after a moment you got hold of yourself and said, "I don't always cry. Sometimes I tell jokes. Do you know how to make holy water? Boil the hell out of it!" The people did not know whether to laugh or cry!

. . .

At the end of the conference, when I was trying to thank the people, I thanked you and Henri too. When I said that you and I lived in the same house for many years, but finally moved into separate houses, you yelled from behind me, "Thank God for that!!!" It brought the house down! . . .

From the outset, Bill wanted his best friend and our pastor, Henri, to bless his life-story-book at a community worship service, so as soon as it was finished, the date was set. Many of Bill's friends were present. Henri called Bill into the centre of the room, took the large three-ring binder full of letters from Bill and pictures of him, and holding it in front of him, spoke to Bill about the importance of his history.

> You were the first person to come and live in our community, Bill, so you are an important founder of Daybreak. It would be hard for us to imagine what Daybreak would be like if you had not been here. You are loved and you are special.
>
> It is also clear that your vocation is to speak to others and tell them about our life at L'Arche, about how we live together and try to support each other. You have a gift to touch people's hearts by sharing your experience of community life. You and I and others have travelled together to many, many groups of people who were waiting to hear "Good News," and to be encouraged. Remember the times you spoke at conferences, told your jokes, and had everyone laughing? You shared some of your difficulties too, and I like the way you spoke of them so simply and without a lot of drama. When I looked out at the people listening to you, I saw

that some of them had tears in their eyes. You have a special gift to meet people, Bill, and to encourage them.

Today we are here to bless your wonderful Life-Story book. To bless someone is to say good things to that person and about that person. Look around you and see how many of your long-term friends are here. Together we want to bless you and bless your life-story because you are important in our lives and we recognize the importance of your life-story. We love you, Bill. Now, you hold your life-story-book while we bless you.

With his friends gathered around, Bill held his book as the blessings were spoken. When it was over, Bill fell sobbing into Henri's arms, unable to contain his mixed emotions. For a long time they stood together. Then, one by one, Bill accepted the congratulations offered by his friends.

Looking through Bill's life-story-book with him, one realizes that this man has no consistent history prior to his sixteenth year of life. In many ways his life-story-book is such a poor and little history, full of huge gaps. One can sit and read the simple words, while Bill, with tears in his eyes, cries, laughs, talks, and claims his story. In doing so, one is touched by the depth and the value, the beauty and the fruitfulness of this unique life.

Henri writes to Bill in his life-story-book:

You remember the "elevator event"? You and I went into the elevator and there were many people standing against the walls not saying a word. As the elevator was moving upwards you broke the silence by saying to your neighbour, looking at his feet, "You could certainly use a shoeshine!" and when your neighbour nervously grinned at your remark, you said, "but I certainly could use one too!" Within a few seconds everybody was talking to one another in such an animated way that people forgot to get off at their floor! I hope you know that you have a gift of creating community on the spot!

. . .

You are a very special man and a very beautiful friend. Be sure that I want to be a good friend to you, too."

With whom do we claim our unique story?

Full of beauty and full of pain, we each have a priceless history with others who have touched us profoundly. We tend to get bogged down in the gaps, blaming people and using our scars as an excuse for not risking ourselves, for not building relationships, creating family and making history together with others.

Bill is a remarkable example for us. Somewhere, because of his trust in friends, he is choosing to draw together his past with all its beauty and all its pain. With a beautiful simplicity he is no longer blaming others, but he is finding the courage to step through some of the pain and take responsibility for his life and his vocation. He is choosing to move ahead with new-found confidence that his life is good and his friendships are bearing fruit in the lives of other people. These choices disempower those who would make him believe that his life and his gifts are not important. In his inimitable way, Bill would want to encourage us by telling us that "the tea bag shows its strength only when it sits for awhile in hot water!"

Peter

V

A PLACE TO CONFRONT FEAR

When we find ourselves in new and unfamiliar situations, when we see a spider or a snake, when we cannot speak the language, when we waken after a bad dream, we know raw fear. It grips us and renders us helpless. When we board an airplane, we may try to tell ourselves that hundreds and thousands of people get on airplanes every day and there is no need to fear, but we do so nonetheless. We try to persuade ourselves that we are not in danger, but our fear is not susceptible to our reason. We grasp the hand of a friend, but fear seems to have a tighter grip!

Fear is powerful and real. Once it gains a foothold in our lives, it becomes a cruel taskmaster, robbing us of our freedom to enjoy simple pleasures. It is irrational. All the arguments in the world cannot talk us out of it. Fear makes us painfully insecure, upsets our equilibrium, and covers us like a dark and threatening cloud.

Home with friends, Peter grapples with fear

It is a gift that Peter, who loves community and has the ability to live it well, came when Daybreak was just starting, because he gave so much to the spirit of this new community in the Toronto area. He loves people, events, church, dances, parties, vacations, and guests for supper. People love him when they experience his welcome and his enthusiasm. When the celebration is over and everyone is tired and glad to be going home, Peter remarks, "That was so good! I could stay all night.", then he looks sideways at his neighbour and asks, "Do you think we could do it again tomorrow?" Peter makes community living believable.

When he was small, he was perhaps too well-protected from danger, and thus from a certain growth. Peter never went out alone as a child, and as a young adult all his personal choices were made for him by others. His world was very small, very safe, very contained.

He did not go to school, but learned to read, to write and to play the piano at home. When he started piano lessons, his ear was so good that teachers saw no value in teaching him to read music. They encouraged him to continue on his own. Later he taught himself how to do it, but because he didn't have teachers, Peter was never encouraged in his playing, and lost confidence in himself.

It seems that Peter worked hard to please his parents and his grandmother, virtually the only references during his childhood. When he was eighteen and his mother died, Peter lost his loving, safe, small home and was placed in a large facility where he lived with two hundred other men with disabilities. The shift was traumatic and left its mark on Peter's heart, mainly because his loving, long-term relations were suddenly gone and his heart was broken. Each week in the institution he had as many as seventeen people to whom he was directly accountable, and this confused him and made him very anxious. He wanted to please them, but there were simply too many people with too many demands. Peter can speak of his fear, apprehension and loneliness, and of all the desires of his heart for affection, love, family, fruitfulness, and home. "I was always afraid in the hospital. Some of the men were quite angry and violent and I wished I could help them, but I was afraid they would hit me. When we were all together in the recreation room, it was noisy because the terrazzo floors and fold-away chairs echoed, so that I was frightened. I was even afraid to look at some of the people because I thought they would be mad at me if I did. Sometimes when I looked at TV and saw people in their living rooms, I longed to have a safe home like that, with only a few family members there, and with carpets on the floor."

Peter's father and step-mother wanted the best for him and, realizing his unhappiness, were among the first parents to visit Daybreak when it opened in 1969. They sought admission for him and he was the second person to come. Peter speaks of his gratitude for them when he tells people about his home, always adding, "I'm so glad my parents read an article in the paper about Daybreak and helped me to get here."

As well as his gifts, Peter brought to Daybreak his anxieties and his irrational fears of people, of being judged or criticized, and of having to make choices. It is difficult for him to be addressed directly, given instructions, corrected, or made aware of something about his appearance, and it is similarly difficult for him to make decisions, mainly because he has little experience with people and few relational skills. Living in the community these many years where we try to encourage people to be as independent as possible, to learn new skills, to learn to make choices and to live by them has never been simple or easy for Peter. He fears and hates being confronted, and consistently tries to justify his behaviour by saying, "Well, many people get confused, don't they?"

Even after ten years with friends at Daybreak, Peter's deep insecurity was evident when we wanted to offer him a choice about his living situation. We had a new home near the centre of town where he could independently shop and walk to work. It was also much smaller and more comfortable than the home he was living in, which we felt would be a big attraction for him. When asked if he would consider moving there, his answer was clear: "No thank you. I'm happy where I am." This was true, but there were so many more advantages for Peter at the new home. When he was faced with a decision, however, he simply could not listen. When we realized that it was fear that was preventing him from making the choice, we invited Peter to visit the home for one month, after which he could return to his former one. He accepted, and he absolutely loved it! One day, towards the end of that month, after he raved about how much he liked living there, we asked him about the possibility that he might choose to live there permanently. We wanted him to choose. At once, he replied, "No, I'm OK in the other home." So, later in the same month we invited Peter to extend the visit and stay another month, after which he could return to the old home. He happily accepted. We followed this routine for three or four more months until Peter, looking sideways, remarked, "I guess I must have made the choice, right?" Indeed he had, and this indirect decision was one of many that was breaking down the power of his fear.

Escalators have been one of the biggest chal-lenges for him. It may be perceptual, but he cannot seem to get onto them. We have often stood together at the top and then at the bottom, trying. He waits and watches the steps as they emerge and slowly form, but he cannot take the step that puts him on. We have tried counting them as they came out, hoping on the count of ten to go, but it never works! We have tried starting from a distance, out of sight of the escalator, to walk and to keep walking right onto the step, but he freezes at the last moment.

After many, many years in the community, one day Peter actually took the initiative to ask if we could practice getting on and off the escalator, because he really wanted to be able to do it. In a large shopping mall, we began! He walked right up to the step and he stopped. We went back again and again, but he couldn't do it. We studied the escalator, watching the steps emerge and form, and we talked about how carefully designed they were and how safe! Then we tried again, to no avail! He was afraid, embarrassed, occasionally able to laugh at himself, but most often saying, "Well, many people have trouble with escalators, don't they?" We continued for more than two hours, and when it was clear we were failing badly, I asked Peter if he would be willing to close his eyes and trust me to walk with him and gradually lead him onto the step so that he would not fall. Amazingly, he said, "Yes". He steeled himself, took my arm and away we went, walking first in circles at the foot of the escalator, and finally onto the first step. What joy! What a feeling of accomplishment! He clapped for himself all the way to the top as he bathed in another big victory over his fear!

Peter was a steady worker at the sheltered workshop, ARC Industries, for twenty-five years. Others found regular work outside the workshop, but Peter felt insecure and refused all offers of support for more than ten years. Then, without telling anyone, he read an ad in the local paper and phoned the local hospital giving his name and telling the lady that he wanted to apply for the job, advertised in the paper. She very kindly told him that the position was filled, but she also encouraged him to continue looking. Because of this encouragement, he gathered his courage and announced to the people at Daybreak that he had made the call and that he wanted help to find a *real* job. His determination covered his fear! Wayne, a former businessman, responded to his call for help.

The local lawyers' office invited Wayne and Peter to draw up a job description around delivering mail and telephone messages, tidying the cafeteria, and putting the mail through the postage meter. Peter began with enthusiasm, and was welcomed and appreciated for his warmth and his good humour. They genuinely wanted him to succeed. But he couldn't master the postage meter. Trying to calculate the right amount for each letter and adjust the numbers in the three columns to reflect the correct postage was more than he could do. Wayne worked hard trying to teach Peter, by posting sticky notes with instructions all over the machine and leaving Peter to practice, but when alone, Peter faltered, losing confidence. He couldn't get it. After three weeks and no progress, Peter was feeling very discouraged. Wayne called Pitney-Bowes, the company which owned the postage meter, and he talked about the problem. They very generously lent them a machine with larger numbers, and Peter began again to practice. In frustration and nervousness, he'd say, "I'm doing my best," and, "Well, many people have trouble with postage machines, don't they?"

One day, at the end of the month, when Wayne came in and asked, "How are you doing?", Peter answered, "Fine, thank you!" And he was! Instead of setting the new numbers while the old were still showing, Peter, by never giving up, had devised a way to clear all the old numbers to zero with his thumb, and then to set each new number from there! Peter held this position in good standing for three years, leaving fear behind and learning many new office skills as well as confidence in himself. He now holds another job in a local publishing house.

For twenty-five years, in winter and summer, supported by us or not, Peter has gone every Thursday and every Sunday to St. John's Anglican Church where he sings in the choir. It is a small congregation and Peter is well-known by most of the members. Once when a dispute erupted between the choir and the minister, the members decided neither to robe nor to sing. Peter was anxious at first until he took some time to make a decision for himself. Fully robed every Sunday for the next many months he sat alone in the choir and sang with the congregation. When someone asked him about the situation he very quietly responded, "I know that people are upset with each other. I am sorry about that and I feel nervous because I feel the tension. I have no hard feelings though, for the minister or for the other choir members, and I sing in the choir to praise God. I thought about it and I decided to come on Sunday, to robe and to sing. I pray for everyone, too." His quiet presence alone in the choir, week after week, was a powerful witness to the minister, the choir, and the members of his congregation.

Peter gets up every morning and faces so many challenges to go beyond his fear. Through all the days and months and years, he has continued in a peaceful, non-aggressive way to live and to enjoy what life offers to him, refusing to be bound more than necessary by the limitations of his past. He is a wonderful community-builder. Right in the midst of it he finds support to stand up and take his place, where he can offer friendship, care and welcome to others along the way. He does not stop to become depressed when he fails, nor does he need to blame someone else for his difficulties. Committed to live his life beyond his fear, Peter's life is both full and fruitful.

Well, many people struggle with fear, don't they?

It's true! Subtle fears govern our actions and decisions and, not wishing to be known or judged to be afraid, we cannot ask or welcome support. Sometimes we are afraid of being afraid!

Fear is never more powerful than when we are alone, and fear is weakened when we are together. Together we rob fear of its power by giving and receiving support to face it, grapple with it, and act in spite of it. Together, not alone, we find the strength to take the step that puts us onto the escalator of confidence, and together we clap for ourselves as we ride into new freedom and fulfillment.

VI

A PLACE TO DISCOVER OUR BEAUTY

Our society gives us a strong message that beauty and physical appearance are terribly important. We spend billions of dollars every year on fashion, make-up, and hair-styling. In the corporate world, in politics and entertainment, there is an image: thin, appropriate height, smooth skin, coloured and "styled" hair, fresh-smelling, well "made-up," and "chic". Trying to live up to it, we cover the exquisite "ravages of time" with hair dye, transplants, false teeth, make-up, and face-lifts. If, through no fault of our own, we are overweight, too tall or too short, or marred in any way, we instantly lose respect and our potential for acceptance and success.

We judge ourselves and others by appearances, often disregarding as useless that which looks to be less than our standard of "normal" or "perfect." This judgement not only bypasses the real person, who is

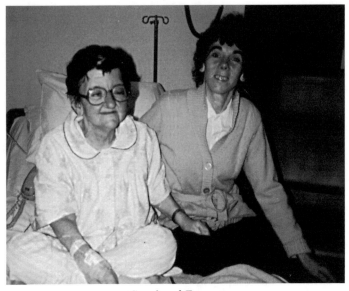

Carol and Frances

more than a body, but it also wounds and kills the small and fragile self-image within each of us that longs for affirmation and acceptance.

Encouraged, Carol welcomes the truth of her life

Born with a disfigured face, with disfigured hands and an intellectual disability, Carol was placed at birth in a facility housing 4,000 disabled people. It was her home for forty-two years before she came to live in the L'Arche community of Erie, Pennsylvania.

With the help of twenty slides, Carol told her life story to a group of more than a hundred and fifty students at the University of Marquette in Milwaukee several years later. She spoke about growing up in the institution where family and long-term, consistent relationships, were absent.

From the time I was very little, people teased me about my face and about my eyes being slanted and so far apart, so I always knew there was something wrong with me. But in the hospital [her name for the institution], if no one teased me, I forgot, because there were few mirrors and I seldom saw myself.

During my life there I made some very good friends, but it was hard to stay together because things could change very fast. Suddenly, one of my friends would disappear and if I asked, I would learn that she had been placed in another hospital! Or, our hospital, without telling us, would plan changes, so that I could be moved from one part of the hospital to another, without preparation or time to say good-bye. That was very hard for me, because I loved my friends and it hurt me to not see them any more. I was sad in myself for a long time after something like that. It took a lot of time for me to make new friends!

Sometimes I used to hide my shoes or to do something else that was bad, but not very bad. I did it because I wanted so desperately to hear my name. In the hospital I sometimes felt scared inside, and the only thing that would calm me was to hear my name. People there didn't say my name very often, but if I hid my shoes, I would hear the staff asking, "Where are Carol's shoes?"; "Carol, where did you put your shoes?"; "Carol has lost her shoes again!"; "Have you seen

Carol's shoes?" It was a little game I played because it helped me to feel safe.

Since the time I was a very small girl, I was always ashamed of my hands, and I did everything to hide them. We had no clothes of our own in the hospital, so every day I had to ask for a dress or a blouse with big pockets. Then I could hide my hands. You see, (and Carol held up her hands), I only have three fingers which are very big, crooked and bony. It looks like two or three fingers got stuck together into one! People who saw my hands made fun of them or were shocked, and sometimes they would not shake hands with me. If we ever sang or performed, staff always put me in the front row because I am so short, but I hated being in the front row because we had to keep our hands at our sides, and I was ashamed of my hands. If they took a video of our performance and played it back, I always asked to be excused, pretending I had to go to the washroom, because I did not want to see myself, especially my hands.

I liked the chapel, the worship and the pastor at the hospital. When I was in my twenties, the pastor asked me if I would read one of the Scripture readings for the Worship Service. Of course I said No. Not long after, he asked me again, and again I refused. After several attempts to get me to read in the service, he called me into his office and he asked me why I would not read. I told him, "I won't read because to read I have to hold the book and I am ashamed of my hands." Then and there he talked to me saying that my hands, though different from other people's hands were good hands to be used to help myself and others and to be of service. He reminded me that I was able to take care of the children at the hospital with my hands and for that I could be thankful to the God who had made my hands and who wanted me to have these hands! I went away and I did not forget his talk. I thought about what he had said to me – for about two years! Finally, one day I walked right into his office and I said, "OK, I will read." From then on, I was not so ashamed of my hands.

Carol then spoke to the university students about her coming to L'Arche and her life there.

When I was forty-two years old, I moved to the L'Arche community of Erie, Pennsylvania. and the first words I said to anyone were, "Don't put that mirror in my room!"

"But why not?" asked an assistant who was moving my things, to which I answered, "Because I will never look in it!"

When he said, "But why would you never look in the mirror?" I told him, "Because I hate myself and I will never look at myself in the mirror. That's why!"

The assistant told me that he thought it would be good to put the mirror there anyway, because someday I just might want to look at myself. I knew that I wouldn't, but I let him do it anyway. Then, one day, about two years later, I decided to look at myself in the mirror! I did, and do you know what I said to myself? I said, "You know, you aren't so bad after all!"

I always had a dream about meeting my family. I remember that when I was little, my father used to come and see me, but I had no real memory of my mother coming. One day, I talked about my dream – to meet my family after all these years. I also said that I was afraid they would not like me because of the way I looked. I do not know how it happened, but people at L'Arche found my family. They lived in Florida. For almost two years they all wrote letters back and forth about me and about our fears to see each other after all these years. I never thought it would happen, but it did. I made the trip to Florida, on the plane, by myself, and I met my mother when I was 47 years old! My father seemed happy to see me and they invited me to come and visit again. I've made several visits to spend time with my family.

After ten years of living in a household with many other people, another dream came true and I was able to move with my friend, Frances, into our own apartment, which was the upstairs of a house. (I had always wanted to become more independent but I never thought I could do it.) The landlady lived downstairs and she was wonderful. We helped her with her shopping and with the garden sometimes. We did almost everything for ourselves, but an assistant came twice a week to support us and to help us do menus, shopping lists, cheques, and social activities. When I saw that I could do it, I was able to encourage others to try it, knowing how much they wanted to live on their own without "staff" always telling them what to do. It was great.

Three years after moving into the apartment, I talked with Lydia, the Director at L'Arche, about my desire to leave the sheltered workshop and get a *real* job. The interview was scary, but I very badly wanted normal work. When the man in charge of the interview asked me, "What can you do with those hands?" I said right back, "You tell me what the job is, and I will tell you whether or not I can do it with my hands." Do you know? I got the job! Now I work at a coffee shop. I wipe the tables and I carry the dishes to the dishwasher. And I get a regular salary, too.

My life now is good. I am happy. I love my home, my family and my community. I want to live for a very long time.

Carol told her story so simply and candidly that the students were profoundly moved. It was a story that traced her journey through shame and rejection, to self-acceptance and wholeness.

Unfortunately, Carol's dream to live a long life was never realized. After eleven years in L'Arche she was diagnosed with a very aggressive form of cancer. She gave up her job, lost her apartment and moved back into a household to receive the help she needed. It was difficult to witness her struggle, as her gains became her losses once again. It was not sad though, because Carol, with the help of a loving community, remained determined and passionate. She exceeded predictions about her life expectancy by over one year. When the hospice nurses came to visit, Carol was out shopping or visiting! She was actually bedridden only a few weeks prior to her death. Her community was in awe of her acceptance of her illness because she never let it hold her down. She died surrounded by her friends and she is remembered as a courageous woman. Carol found some happiness, she gave love and received it, and she learned to love herself as she was!

Who is fairest of us all?

When I visited a home for disabled children in Cleveland, Ohio many years ago, a nurse showed me the facility and introduced me to the children. We came to a crib and I saw the very small body of a child. As my eyes moved to look at the face, the nurse was removing a large, lace cloth that covered the child's enormous head. My eyes took everything in at once; a hydrocephalic child with a tiny body, spindly arms and legs, minuscule fingers and toes and a head that was three times the size of a normal person's head. I was caught off guard between revulsion and pity when I heard the nurse, speaking with such affection and love, "This is Gloria. Isn't she beautiful!"

We receive the sense of our identity, not by ourselves, alone, but by those who love us and who affirm us in our beauty. Committed to one another in the broken and blessed body of humanity, we are privileged to recognize and call forth beauty, talents, and gifts that lie hidden and dormant behind physical appearance and below seeming limitations. In committed relationships we may also find the safety and the courage to look at our own reflections in the mirror and remark with Carol, "You know, you aren't so bad after all!"

David

VII

A PLACE TO HOLD LONELINESS

There is a story about a young priest who, looking into the garden one day saw a vision of Jesus. Not knowing what to do, he asked the pastor, "Jesus is standing in the garden. What should I do?"

The pastor, not knowing either, called the bishop. "Bishop, Jesus is standing in our garden. What should we do?"

The Bishop called the Cardinal, who finally contacted the elderly, Italian Pope. "Pope, Jesus is here and is standing in our garden. What should we do?"

There was a long pause before the Pope finally gave the answer: "Look busy!"

Keeping busy at work, taking in the latest movies or concerts, keeping abreast of friendships, travelling, or dining in the best restaurants only takes the edge off the little cry that continually echoes at the centre of our hearts. It is a painful cry that becomes louder when we are alone or when there is less activity. Because we don't know what to do, we mostly choose to look busy, distract ourselves, and pretend that it is not there at all. But it does not go away, and it is a persistent cry for love and intimacy. Our little hearts are deeply lonely and we yearn for more than a life of entertainment and busyness.

David doesn't want a raise!

When Daybreak opened David's mother was just coming to terms with the fact that she had to try to find David a home of his own. Her preference would have been to keep him with her and to help him to live with his intellectual disability by giving her life to care for him. But she felt that he had a right to find his own life away from her, just as her other children had, so she placed him in Daybreak in 1969. It cost her greatly to place David in the care of others, but her fidelity to him over the next fifteen years before her death was not lost. He needed her love to help him find his own life, to grow and mature into a man of stature.

Because of David's very strong experience of family life he was insecure when he moved away, and the deeper desires of his heart began to surface. What became obvious and remains obvious to this day is that David would like to be married. He wants communion with another person, emotional communion and physical communion, because he is very physical. David longs for the comfort and security of an intimate relationship, which is difficult to sustain when one suffers from an intellectual disability. Most probably David will never have a life-partner. His yearning to be touched and to be held, to have an experience of fullness and of ecstasy will, most likely, never be fully realized. This is the unrelenting suffering of his life.

David lives this deep suffering in his home and in a community where men and women assistants have been coming and going for the past twenty five years. Without trying, David has fallen in love with more than one of the beautiful young women who has come to assist and live in the community. Some of the women, trying not to hurt David, responded to his signs of affection in ways that seemed to lead him on. His heart was taken. Then, inevitably, that woman would become involved in an intimate relationship with another assistant, or would leave the community to pursue a personal journey, in which case David was left behind to deal with his losses. Occasionally he became angry and disagreeable, but more often he was simply depressed. Mysteriously, and without chasing distractions, he is learning to live his personal vulnerability without blaming anyone, without taking it out on others in the home, and without drowning in it himself.

With his handicap, David cannot "look busy" or run in the fast lane, so he loses the comfort of some of today's distractions. He does not play sports, does not watch TV, or enjoy movies. David enjoys smoking a pipe and likes to go for a walk or out for lunch with Joe or Lori who are his friends. As they enjoy the time together, David inevitably asks, "Lori, how long have we known each other? Ten years?" He enjoys having a cup of tea with a friend, and he will sit in the living room when we have a house meeting or when we are just talking together. He likes long meals where the conversation is not too intellectual. He enjoys being invited to the men's group to share and listen with others about affectivity and sexuality. He has many questions about people coming to the community and why they are coming, about what happened to someone who is ill, and the whereabouts of people who were here twenty years ago and whose names he still remembers. Being connected to people in these small ways holds David's heart in enough security to allow him to express his beautiful gifts of care and humour in the community.

He likes to welcome people, and he takes visitors for a walk, asks many questions about their personal history, and then leads them on about his life as a paratrooper in the army, or as a priest! They come back shaking their heads, not knowing what to believe, but few forget their "walk with David."

He enjoys answering the phone, and inevitably has a small conversation with the caller even if he or she is not calling for him!

Caller: "Hello, may I please speak to Sue Mosteller?"

David: "Who's this?"

Caller: "This is Mary calling. Is Sue there?"

David: "Oh, hello Mary. Are you a friend of Sue's?"

Caller: "Yes. Sue and I have been friends for a long time."

David: "Good! Where did you meet Sue?"

Caller: "We met at a retreat quite a long time ago. Tell me, is Sue there?"

David: "Well, what did you want to talk to Sue about, tonight, Mary?"

Caller: "We are getting together next week and I'm trying to find out if she can pick me up."

David: "Oh, that's nice. Well, Sue isn't home right now. Do you want to leave your number?"

And so it goes. So many times, David has not quite been able to write the name or all the numbers for the return call, but I can always identify the person because he has so much data from his personal conversation with the caller!

One day when the phone rang and David answered, it was the long distance operator.

"Hello, I have a collect call for anyone from Joe Egan. Will you accept the charge?" (Joe was David's friend and an assistant in his house who had gone to Boston for the weekend.)

"No," answered David, "Joe's not home."

"No, no," the operator protested, "this is a collect call *from* Joe Egan for anyone. Will you accept the charge?"

"Nope!" said David with authority. "Joe is in Boston."

Pause.

Joe Egan, in Boston, trying to help, said, "Dave, it's me, Joe. Say Yes to accept the charge."

The operator moved swiftly, "Excuse me sir, please do not speak to your party unless you wish to pay for this call!"

A longer pause.

Then David queried. "Oh, Joe, there's a call here for you. What should I do?"

David has a wonderful gift of humour. As four of us were driving to a meeting in Erie, Pennsylvania, I tried to make conversation by saying that I was lucky to be able to fit my guitar into one of the other cars. When no one responded I continued, saying, "Maybe, at the meeting, they will ask me to play." No response. "You know," I said, "they probably heard that I was taking lessons, so they might ask me to go up on the stage and perform for everyone." Silence. With one last try I said, "I can play 'Long, Long Ago', you know." After a perfect pause, David from the back seat muttered, "Yes, and you should play it far, far away!"

On another occasion when Dave and I were sitting together in the living room late at night having a cup of tea I said, "Oh Dave, I am so tired.

Do you think you could carry me upstairs to bed?" to which David replied, "I could, but I'd need a crane!"

Another day in the car, David, began asking in a serious voice, "Sue, will you ever go back to the convent and . . . ," followed by a long pause. I waited, curious to know his question. He began again, "Sue are you going to go back to the convent someday and . . . ." Silence. I waited. A third time he started, "Sue, will you ever go back to the convent and . . . become a woman again?"

David's life revolves around home. He lived faithfully for eighteen years in the same house, welcoming and sending off in that time more than a hundred assistants and fellow core members. Every day he suffers the loss of his dream and every day he calls the people in his home to be with him, to be home, to take a walk or to stay together at the table or in the living room. Often his call goes unnoticed, but David remains, calling, by his life, for presence and communion.

His strong faith life not only sustains him, but helps others. His Emmanuel Church Community is important to him and the people all know him and recognize him for his fidelity over the past twenty five years. Each weekday morning he attends the 8:30 a.m. worship in the Daybreak chapel. He is an active member of the Daybreak Pastoral Team and works on the committee planning a new prayer house and chapel for Daybreak. The meetings may be too long or involved for him, too based on paper which he cannot read, but David is present, making comments and asking questions, and inviting people to greater simplicity and presence.

He loves his boss, Joe, in the wood-working shop, and it is Joe who told the following story about one of the more important moments in his life at Daybreak. It was noon and the men were getting ready to go to their regular Friday lunch at the Richmond Hill Diner.

"I was feeling low, exhausted, and with no energy, and the last thing I wanted to do was to go to lunch with everyone. Because it is such an important part of the week though, I decided that I would go, so I got into the car and slouched behind the wheel, waiting for the men to get in. Dave was in the seat behind me, and while we were waiting, he began to massage my shoulders and back. 'Oh Dave,' I said, 'that feels so good! If you continue to do that, I'll give you a raise!' Dave went on working for a moment before replying, 'I don't want a raise, Joe. I just want to be with you.'"

Sometimes, because of his broken heart and unfulfilled sexuality, his life is tipped over and he wears his heart on his sleeve, unable to hide his distress at a pain that is not going to be "fixed." After thirteen years living safely in the community and with enormous, faithful support from his family, one day he asked very seriously, "Sue, who will look after me, who will care for me when my mother dies?" He longs to be unique for someone. Yet his pain is not all there is. Fortunately for him and for so many others who have been touched by him, David chooses to live despite and beyond the ever-present cry of his heart. His life, with all its grief, radiates gentleness, humour and simplicity.

Our hearts don't want a raise

David's heart is both unique and universal! His yearnings are a reflection of mine and yours. Pain, whether from a broken heart, broken sexuality, loneliness, loss, abuse or grief, has tremendous power to dominate and ruin our lives! Pain snatches and swallows our potential for the comfort and joy of simple, loving and life-giving relationships. When our hearts are broken, we don't need distraction or money, but friends and community. We need people to elicit our gifts and help us to feel good about ourselves despite our losses. We need friends who know our value beyond present vulnerability and grief.

Relationships in community life hold us with our broken hearts and draw us away from a life of distraction and quiet despair. Family is a place where our experience touches the depth of David's wisdom: "I don't want a raise, Joe. I just want to be with you."

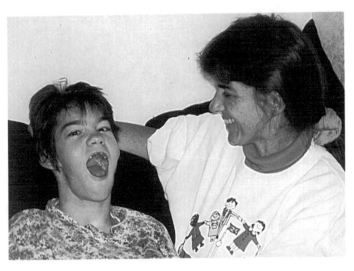

Tracy and Paula

VIII

A PLACE TO SURRENDER CONTROL

One of the big plusses of living alone is the opportunity to have full freedom and control over our own lives. Until it begins to slip away through accident or illness, we are unaware of how desperately we cling to control, consciously or unconsciously. We experience difficulty with authority. We do not want to be dependent on others and we like to make our own decisions about how we spend our time, how we dress, what we eat, the entertainment we enjoy, and the company we keep.

But dependency is written into our flesh. How quickly we forget that our lives are sandwiched between two primal cries of dependency: the cry of the newborn infant who cannot live if left alone, and the cry of the dying person who is incapacitated and dependent.

Physical and mental disabilities deprive us of a certain control that we normally enjoy, and rob us of some of our capacities to make decisions for our lives and to implement them. Living together also divests us of total control because we have to give up and give in to others much of the time. Responsibility and commitment require that we surrender control in service to others.

The journey to surrender control is difficult and long. We naturally resist and build barriers to separate ourselves from those who would help us see our limitations and promote our wholeness. The journey to interdependence is complicated, because we easily swing between the seduction of a selfish, independent lifestyle on the one hand, or we lose our balance and fall into destructive dependencies on the other. We are wise if we find good teachers who point a way by example through the narrow passage which leads to healthy surrender.

Tracy lets herself be accompanied on her voyage to surrender

Meeting Tracy is to meet her eyes! They find you and gather you into her person. They shine. They never look too long, but turn aside after an interval, and then return to welcome you again. Meeting Tracy, you have to bend down because she sits in her wheelchair or lies on the futon on the floor in the living room. You bend over her, and you may have to wait for almost a minute before she can coordinate all the necessary muscles to lift her head from its downward position to look into your eyes.

She may not be able to do it alone, and may have to accept the hand of the assistant on her forehead, gently helping her to mobilize and bring her head into an upright position.

When you meet Tracy, you are primarily conscious of the way her body holds her prisoner and of how much she cannot do. She is unable to sit up by herself, much less to stand or walk! She struggles to make the slightest movements with her contorted, spastic, and uncontrollable body. On the futon on her living room floor there is nowhere to fall and she can move freely without much risk! She cannot feed herself nor perform any of her own self-care. At first you might be tempted to say, "What a pity!" But within a very few minutes you would have to add, "Wow! What eyes! She sure is alive in there!"

Though Tracy has no words, her friend and assistant Paula, as well as many other friends and assistants, understand her language. Paula asks in words, "Tracy, can I give you some chocolate ice cream?" and she responds with her smile. It may take time to answer, but if she wants the ice cream, she smiles, sometimes with a little sound of laughter, and if she doesn't smile (which is never the case with chocolate ice cream!) the answer to the question is No.

Tracy is aware of everyone and of what is said in conversation. She reacts when the names of her friends are mentioned or when something funny is said. Assistants who bathe her or sit with her during her meal sometimes make Tracy their confidant because she listens, she hears, and she carries their stories. When old friends write or phone to announce they are coming to visit, Tracy lets out a yelp of delight.

Tracy is unable, by herself, to play pranks or jokes, so Paula asks, "Trace, do you think we should initiate Randy, the new assistant?" Tracy's head goes back, her mouth opens wide, and her smile is unmistakable! Paula takes her hand, puts it on the full syringe of water, and as Randy passes by, together they aim and shoot! Randy screams and blames Paula. Paula blames Tracy. Tracy roars with laughter as her body shakes with delight.

Mealtimes were happy times for Tracy, even if she enjoyed playing games and controlling events by not opening her mouth for the meat and vegetables in order to move more quickly to dessert, her favourite! When Paula fed her, there was a three-step progression: no "Boost" (a delicious and nutritious chocolate drink) without meat and vegetables first, then no dessert (pudding, also chocolate) without Boost!

A few years ago, Tracy's eating began to present problems, and the cause was not immediately evident. Some days she could eat a whole bowl in half-an-hour, while other days, she could only take three spoonfuls in an hour! Coughing spasms began sporadically, then became regular whenever she was eating. She began to lose weight. Tests confirmed that the muscles that helped her to swallow had deteriorated so that she was aspirating her food, with much of it going into her lungs. Her cough was not strong enough to bring the food back, so it sat there for days, choking her and making her very uncomfortable. With time, feeding was so painful that she ate very little and was steadily losing weight. Doctors showed Tracy, her family, and the people of Daybreak the test results on the screen, where all could see exactly where the food was going. They gave the prognosis that Tracy's condition would get worse and not better. The only thing to help Tracy, they said, was for her to accept a feeding tube, and from then on to refrain from taking food by mouth. She was told that, in order to insert the tube and begin the new feeding regime, she would have to remain in the hospital for three days. Tracy was part of the whole process and with others, she said yes to this direction. It was only her first yes. Paula accompanied her on this "voyage of surrender."

After the surgery she had a liquid drip that gave her nourishment steadily for twenty-four hours, but she couldn't manage it and was sick to her stomach most of that day. She was uncomfortable, too, because she loves to lie on her stomach, but the new button for the feeding tube was there; it could not take the pressure, so she had to lie on her back.

The next week-and-a-half were terrible for Tracy. She remained in the hospital, throwing up, crying, tense, restless and very uncomfortable. Doctors would not let her go home until her condition stabilized, so Daybreak people stayed with her around the clock trying to comfort and support her as the agony of her rigid, thrashing body caused her to cry out day and night.

On one of these nights near the end of the second week, Tracy's friend Paula began to reach her own limits while she watched Tracy in such misery. Along with countless others in the course of the week, Paula had tried to explain to Tracy how important it was for her to relax, but Trace was not listening. Thinking Tracy would hear it better from hospital staff, Paula had asked the night nurse to come in and explain. Nothing helped, as Tracy's body remained stiff and flailed in anguish.

Paula laid down the law! "Tracy, you have to begin to relax. If you continue this thrashing, I am going to leave and you will be alone." Of course Tracy continued and Paula realized that she couldn't leave! But it was three a.m. and Paula was close to the end of her patience. She tried another way.

"You need to settle down, Tracy," she said with authority. "I care about you, and I do not know what to do to help you. Right now I need some space, so I am going to walk out of here for a time. I will be back, but while I'm gone, please think about what you can do." When she returned twenty minutes later Tracy was still thrashing.

"Tracy, I cannot stand to watch this." she said with frustration. Tracy cried and thrashed. Paula then sat her up and held her in her arms and began to cry, saying, "Tracy, help me understand what is going on. I do not know."

At that moment, held in Paula's arms, Tracy's body fell limp and she began to sob. Paula realized that it was the first time she had asked Tracy anything. She had been telling her, the whole time, what she had to do, but she had never invited Tracy to share her anguish. "It was not conscious on my part," says Paula, "but that moment was very important to both of us.. My pain seemed to touch hers and hers certainly touched mine."

After a while Paula asked, "Are you upset?" and Tracy, more relaxed, followed Paula's lips with her eyes. Paula went on slowly, "Can we talk about it? (Pause) Are you in pain? (Pause) Are you sad? (Pause) Are you angry?" When she said the word "angry," Tracy emitted a loud wail and her body crumpled completely. Then she let out a small sound and smiled.

Then they really talked! Paula named the feelings while Tracy smiled or not in response. When she said yes they stopped and were silent together. Tears ran down Tracy's face when her emotions were named.

Paula: "You are feeling angry because you can no longer eat and enjoy your food."

Tracy: a smile.

Paula: "You know what this means and you do not like it. You are grieving"

Tracy: a sound and a smile.

Paula: "This is one more place in your life where you have lost control, and you hate it."

Tracy: another sound, another smile.

Paula: "Tracy, you are perfectly right to be grieving and in so much pain! I am here and I encourage you to *feel* the pain. You are such a courageous woman!"

Tracy: a very gentle smile and a look of trust.

Not long after that Tracy fell into a deep sleep. Three days later, she was released from the hospital. She cannot speak about her voyage to surrender, but in the next year she made that journey through anger and resistance to acceptance and peace.

Today, almost three years later, she has four meals a day through her feeding tube and nothing, with the exception of an occasional taste of chocolate, by mouth. Every day, when asked, she says yes to come to the dinner table to be with us as we eat. Courageously, she watches, she smells the food, and she relaxes with the flow of the dinner conversation.

Tracy has no hope that her body will change or that her condition will improve. She will always need people to support her to live and move. It seems unfair that one, young person has had to give over so much. One wonders from what depths she draws the strength to integrate and accept such radical limits and to welcome the gift of her life and the opportunity to share it with others. Her eyes and her persistent efforts to welcome, to smile and to listen, reflect that she is at peace with herself and with the world.

We need each other in order to surrender

Our inner breakages, like Tracy's, are not going to get better, are never going to be fixed. The people who broke our hearts, and gave us less physically than we deserved and thus broke us in mind or spirit are never coming back to reverse their action. We are indelibly marked and disabled by the lack of unconditional love in our lives. There are choices we have to make: to sit alone and wallow in the pain, or to surrender and accept the particular help we need to live with our limitations and to enjoy a fruitful and fulfilling life.

Teachers are plentiful. A child, when he or she falls, accepts help to get up! A person with a broken leg accepts a crutch to move about! It may be embarrassing, but teachers like Tracy refuse to be dominated by their limitations. Rather, they live from a source that is deeper than the handicap: they live from their passion for life, relationship and fullness. Paula wrote the following poem to her friend Tracy this year.

Tracy, your friendship
Has taken me into a world I have been unable to explore.
In years gone by
My heart saw no possible way to open the door
Of my house of pain, of hurt, of isolation.
Many people thought my home was filled with only joy and
laughter,
Because they were the only rooms open for viewing
Until I stumbled across friends like you,
Whose sense of acceptance and love
Has called forth my courage
To unveil those haunting,
And daunting rooms of my heart.
They are filled with broken furniture, cobwebs, dust,
Memories, and untold stories.
Tracy, my friend,
I have lots to learn from you
If I am to follow through with my desire
For others to see my "home" –
In the light and in the dark.
Tracy, my friend,
I delight in giving to you,
And I thank you for that which I receive from you.
As our friendship grows
May we learn to hold each other's heart
The way every precious jewel needs to be held –
With support, tenderness and care –
The language of love.

Paula Keleher

IX

A PLACE TO DIE

Recently we had a community meeting to share our experiences of aging, dying, and death. Everyone was invited. Three people said they were afraid and chose not to come. Two others decided not to come, then changed their minds and asked to come only for the first half of the meeting. For all present it was an incredible time of listening and of sharing.

Francis said that he was the one who found his mother when she died. "I came home from work and she was on the floor. I called the neighbour to help."

George shared that when he got older and could no longer live at home, he wanted to go to a nursing home like the one where his father lives. He wants his own room, a TV, a daily newspaper, and good food. When he becomes very ill, he does not want to have many tubes going in and out of his body.

Annie remembered when her "big honey," Frankie, died of Alzheimer's disease in 1979. She cried and said, "Frankie is gone. I loved Frankie, my big honey."

Greg recounted that he did not know what happened to him until his mother told him he had suffered a stroke as a very young child, and that is why his arm is twisted and useless.

Marcie remarked that it was hurtful for her when she had no part in the decisions taken around someone she loved, who was ill and dying in the community.

Joe said that Wendy, a community member and Anglican priest, was so helpful at his father-in law's deathbed during the final hours. She called family members to come around the dying person, Hank, to lay hands on him and pray, and to take time one by one saying good-bye. She also urged family members to leave the sick room for a cup of tea or a short rest.

By being present at this meeting Stephanie felt connected with the experience of her father's death, which was painful for her and was never talked about in her family.

Death is a mystery that affects each one of us. When a loved one dies we suffer loss and grief, or unresolved anger and helplessness, and when we begin to experience our own mortality, we may go through fear or denial. Few are the guides to show us the way to accept and even to welcome our passing from this world to the next.

We needed Bill and Bill needed us

Bill was a perfect gentleman, in possession of himself. His perfectly bald head gleamed over his short frame. On Sundays he wore a fedora to church and his good-quality topcoat over his best blue suit.

At forty-eight years of age he knew himself well, though he was labeled "retarded". Once, as we were standing together in the front entrance of our house, we were greeted by an overly-enthusiastic woman who looked at Bill and announced that she had brought "candies for the kiddies." Bill paused, waited for her to leave and drawled, "I'd rather have beer!"

Bill loved his cigarettes and seemed to revel in breaking the no-smoking-in-the-bedroom rule. He hid the ashtrays in the drawer of his dresser and acted very surprised when they were presented to him as evidence that he was, in fact, smoking. He'd pause, look intently at the ash tray, and then ever so slowly and with perfect composure remark, "Ohhhh, I wonder who was smoking in my room!"

On Saturday mornings he deliberately prolonged his breakfast and kept everyone waiting to plan the morning chores. Cajoling, inviting, asking, demanding, and shouting were all useless means of getting his attention. His jaw was set and only occasionally did he open it wide enough to say, "I hate cleaning!"

Bill had a special charisma around gift-giving. When asked to take him Christmas shopping I was dismayed, first because I have never liked shopping, and secondly because, as a nun, I have little experience. True to form, I sat with Bill the night before the shopping excursion, pen in hand, ready to make the shopping list of all the things he wanted to buy, so that the actual excursion would be brief! I naively thought that we would go, get the gifts quickly, and leave.

"So, Bill," I began efficiently, "What would you like to buy Aunt Ethel for Christmas?" Bill pondered for several moments and drawled, "Let's look and see." I tried again. "What about something for the kitchen" Pot holders? A new apron?" After a moment he replied thoughtfully, "She has a wonderful kitchen. She doesn't need anything for her kitchen." After several more attempts, with nothing on my shopping list and deflated in spirit, I gave up, reluctantly agreeing to "look and see."

At four in the afternoon on December 18 I picked Bill up from work and drove to one of Toronto's biggest malls, assuring myself that it had the most potential for us to "get in, get it, and get out!" I was immediately overwhelmed, set back, and left gasping, as we stepped into the Mall centre where there were lines for Santa and his helpers, Disney characters dancing up and down, music blaring and a huge crowd of shoppers. Bill was energized by it all, and when I said I felt we needed to start with a cup of tea, he seemed dismayed.

While waiting for our tea to come I explained to Bill that it was very crowded in the mall and that we did not have much time, so therefore it would be so helpful if he could think of the kind of gifts he wanted to purchase for his aunts. I suggested, "A sweater, a scarf, a purse?" "My aunts have those things," he said and paused. Then: "Let's look and see."

We went first to Grand and Toy, where the aisles were jammed with shoppers. I showed Bill a decorative Christmas candle which he took and slowly, with careful attention, turned over and over in his hands. Putting it back on the shelf he remarked, "My aunts' living room is green and that candle is red. If they had that in their living room they'd think it was Christmas all year long. Ho! Ho! Ho!"

Similarly I picked up a mug from the shelf and gave it to Bill. He studied it very slowly and replaced it, saying, "My aunts drink their tea from china cups. They don't use mugs in their house!" Similar attempts likewise failed; there was always a reason why something was not a proper gift for his aunts. It was 5:45, and I was still hoping we would be going home for supper. Bill was just warming up!

Around six p.m., while browsing in Simpsons, Bill spotted a jewellery wagon piled high with women's brooches. He was immediately interested and began his quest for an appropriate brooch. In an effort to hurry things along I would present one to Bill with "Look at this one Bill; I think Aunt Helen would love this, don't you?" This would be followed by a two-minute examination of the brooch and a two-minute explanation that Aunt Helen's suit was brown and the bright blue in this particular brooch would clash with her suit. It was seven p.m. by the time we had selected and bought two brooches. I was ready to go home!

Handing me the bag to carry, Bill said very matter-of-factly, "Now I have to shop for Steve and Anne." They were Directors at Daybreak and housemates of Bill. Before proceeding we stopped for supper and Bill asked the waitress to bring two glasses of wine, then looked at me and said, "You brought me shopping and I want to treat you!" It was his perfect gift for me at that moment!

I should have known better than to ask him, as we finished supper, what he had in mind for gifts for Steve and Ann. With the same thoughtfulness and the same drawl he gave the same response, "Let's look and see."

In the drug store Bill stopped before the shaving creams, looking intently at the boxes. When I asked what he saw, he said, "Steve's box is red with a gold seal. I saw it in his bathroom. Can you help me find it?" We did, and we bought it. And the slippers he purchased for Ann had to be blue because, "I saw Ann in her housecoat and it is blue!"

I complained at 8:45 when he said he had to buy one more gift, for Peggy. "Bill," I said with exasperation, "Peggy left Daybreak ten months ago. Why are you buying her a present?" "Because, she was kind to me." he answered with perfect aplomb. Then he proceeded to purchase an Irish mug because Peggy's family came from Ireland.

Alert and active all his life, Bill gloried in his independence. So the beginning of Alzheimer's disease was tremendously difficult for him. As he lost his capacity to speak, he was easily frustrated and threw things down or left in anger. He did not understand what was happening, but he did not want help and he quickly became angry at the person trying to come to his aid.

At night, however, he cried when the assistants turned off the light and left the room. His cries did not stop, but became moans and screams as he tried to tell us that he was afraid to be left alone in the dark. He got up many times in the night, determined to get around on his own, but then he fell and hurt his back and he was in a double agony. We began to take turns sleeping in the room next door, to be available to him during the night. The quality of his life deteriorated so that he was moaning, crying or angry most of the time.

Bill became bedridden within a short period of time, and then, imperceptibly, something began to change. His friend Joe Egan says that Bill made a free choice somewhere inside himself to accept the final stages of his journey.

Did he know that we, as a community, needed a good chronic-care teacher? Did he realize that caring for him is exactly the preparation we needed for others with more severe limitations who would follow him to Daybreak? What insight did he have about the unique gift that would exactly match the current need in his community? We do not know, but Bill appeared to have taken time to "look and see" before he gradually began to move out of his anguish into peace.

In the years that followed, Bill was bed-ridden and lost his mobility, work, social and community life, capacity for holidays, ability to read and write, speech, and ability to feed, bathe and toilet himself. Small bouts of anger and fear early on, gave way to a profound and peaceful acceptance of his journey into total dependency. With each day he became more radiant in his bed.

We made every occasion special because, we said, "This one will surely be Bill's last!" His fiftieth birthday was a bash with all his friends around his bed, with food and gifts, streamers and balloons. And likewise, his fifty-first, fifty-second, up to his fifty-seventh! People gathered around him, spoke into his ear, stroked him, gave gifts, told stories, and sang, while Bill, no longer able to speak, presided from his hospital bed.

For seven years he allowed us to wash, change, and turn him every three hours, as well as to kiss him, talk to him, visit him, move him, and leave him alone for long periods of time while we were busy with others.

We regularly had to meet among ourselves to talk about Bill's care and it was often difficult to be united. He was in a home with other people with special needs, but caring for him was onerous and sometimes took us away from attending to the real needs of others. We had differences about the kind of care that was best for him. One thought we should give him sleeping pills; another countered that this would do nothing for Bill but would make things easier for us! Care-givers suffered when others didn't "care enough," and we accused each other of selfishness in the face of his increasing demands on our time and presence! Bill seemed to know when we were about to explode, so he would remind us that he needed unity, not fragmentation, around him. Without warning, someone would discover him, holding his breath and turning blue! There was a shout, a frenzy to get help to sit him up, a gathering around the bed, a waiting together. Bill was very quiet and very clear! When we were all there, praying and worrying about him, he gave a huge sigh, regained his colour, and offered himself to us in peace again.

At the beginning of his eighth year in bed, Bill began to weaken, was briefly hospitalized, and then came home to die. He died as he had lived those past years, quietly, with his friends around him, and in peace.

After his death we "looked and saw" the beautiful gift that he had bequeathed to us as individuals and as a community. By dying thus, in our midst, he showed us our capacity to care for people with physical as well as intellectual needs. A few years later, with the gift of that confidence, we opened a home for severely physically and intellectually disabled children.

Some pointers from Bill

If he could, Bill, with his slow drawl might tell us the following lessons:

- In caring for someone who is dying, work together and work hard not to judge others on the team. We never know what another person may be suffering and people might be hard to get along with precisely because they are struggling with issues around their own death. A dying person needs unity around them, not fragmentation, so don't judge each other, but work together, giving and receiving the gifts exchanged when someone in your midst is in the final stage of life.

- Together you can do wonders in caring! Alone, you will soon feel burnt out, resentful, tired, overwhelmed and angry, so try to remember how much you need each other. It's not easy and you have to sacrifice your personal space and time, but you become so beautiful when, together, you put yourselves at the service of someone who is weak.

- Live your life as a man or a woman of peace. Make peace with your enemies. Quietly offer to support family members who are burdened with the care of a loved one. When your time comes to die, let your peace be a gift to those who care for you.

Bill

Peter, Elizabeth and Thelus

EPILOGUE

A place to give, but also to receive

When I first came to Daybreak I was physically and emotionally strong; able to carry lots of responsibility and to work hard in building a new community of care and love. I was there to welcome and encourage the more than forty core members who, over the years, came to live in the ten homes of Daybreak. The whole experience was, for me, stimulating and creative, because with some disappointments, I had adequate channels for my energies of love and service. Generous by nature, I poured myself out for all those around me in need. The people and the life sustained me, and my spirit was alive, creative, strong and energetic.

Did I think I was immortal? Perhaps. For the first fifteen years at Daybreak, I was happy and healthy in the service of the kingdom, never considering the possibility of having less energy or of falling apart.

Then I began to experience fatigue and depression that drained me and would not go away. As I became conscious of what was happening, I kept trying to pull myself together, but I couldn't do it. Thinking I should be strong, I didn't tell anyone that I felt very alone and afraid. I wanted a break, but I did not want to be alone, nor did I want to be with other people! Before long I was questioning my ability to cope as I realized that things were going from bad to worse. I found myself in meetings or talking with individuals muttering to myself, "I don't even care what you are saying!" I did care, but my own anguish was too big for me at that moment.

One day during this difficult time, giving talks to assistants in Montreal about personal responsibility, I told them, "*You* are responsible for your own well-being in community. It is imperative that you assume responsibility for your physical and emotional health: find a balanced rhythm of life, take regular exercise, find time for reading and solitude, and work with your fears and angers." Around three o'clock the next morning I awoke with a start, sat straight up in bed, and said to myself, "I am responsible for what is happening to me!" I got up and wrote a letter to the Director of Daybreak asking him to help me. Two days later we began to talk about my situation and I proposed a short-term stay at the Centre Street House for a time of recuperation, because the people there were gentle, trusted friends of mine.

It was Peggy's ability and desire for independence that inspired the Centre Street House to become a house of all core members and no live-in assistants. Annie and Peggy slept in the duplex upstairs while Peter, Thelus and Dave lived in the one downstairs; they managed the home together as one household. Ann, an assistant, came two or three times a week to help them with the bills, the shopping lists, appointments, clothes, and a social calendar, but she lived in her own apartment, away from the home.

Peggy is a wonderful lady, fiercely independent, with many skills, She loved living upstairs with Annie and without assistants! The two of them did their own shopping and banking, cooking and cleaning, and they enjoyed a very busy and full life without waiting to be told by assistants what they had to do. A sports' fan, Peggy purchased a TV for the house, and spent time watching football and baseball, while Annie, who doesn't enjoy sports, came and went alone or with friends. Peg read a lot and built a good library of books on the Royal family and on the Second World War, as well as many mysteries and spy stories. Weekdays Peggy worked in the Daybreak Bakery and later retired to the Senior's Club.

Although she never belonged to the Congregation, Annie boarded for many years with a group of

Anglican nuns in England. When her family immigrated to Canada, Annie came with them and later left her two sisters and her father to bring a sense of community and some beautiful convent characteristics to Daybreak! She is a wonderful, kind person, with a great sense of humor. Her person and her belongings are kept perfectly! She is very discreet and keeps her eyes modestly cast down! She is tidy to the extreme, so that if something is left out of place, she whisks it away quickly to its proper place or out of sight in a drawer somewhere!

Annie does not always have confidence in herself, but she is formidable! When invited to a sports event, she countered, "Oh no, Dear. I don't want to go, Dear. You go, Dear. Not me, Dear!" But when she was pressed, she went along "for the ride." Once there, the assistant invited her to throw some hoops, and Annie responded similarly, "No thanks, Dear. No hoops and loops for me, Dear. You do it, Dear." Again, encouraged and challenged, she conceded, but without enthusiasm and without even looking. One, two, three hoops over the hooks and Annie was a winner!!! On to shooting basketballs and with the same results. After "Oh no, Dear. No balls and baskets for me, Dear. Why don't you do it, Dear?", Annie was persuaded to try. Same posture with no enthusiasm and only glancing a look; one, two, three, and Annie scores again! When complimented that night for four red ribbons, Annie protested, "No way, Dear. I'm not THAT good, Dear. How was your day, Dear?"

David, another member of the Centre Street household, was one of the first people to come to Daybreak twenty-six years ago. Not fond of large crowds, but gifted in one-to-one encounters, David is marvelous. While opening an account with the new bank branch manager, he wanted to know, "Are you new in town?" Then he asked, "Did you know that my grandfather was a bishop?" When he got up to leave, he thanked the manager for helping him and then asked to be introduced to all the tellers in the bank! It was noontime, but the Manager took him to each one and holding up the lines he made the introductions. Fifteen minutes later, when David left the bank, he was on a first name basis with each person there! When David was asked to help with ticket sales to our 25th Anniversary Gala, he got on the phone and sold twenty tickets in one night: to his boss at work, to his minister and church buddies, to the taxi driver who takes him to work! David was overjoyed to be asked to travel and give talks with Henri, our pastor, in the name of L'Arche, and he was not at all shy to move among the crowds of people, answering questions, chatting and making connections. He is amazing!

Peter, whose story is told in another chapter, was David's room-mate at the Centre Street house. He was proud to be invited to live there because he never dreamed that he could manage without the constant support of live-in assistants. Gradually he learned cooking, cleaning, and shopping, plus other social skills, and he was energized by being part of this group that took full responsibility for their home.

Thelus lived downstairs with Peter and Dave. She is a woman of dignity with a desire for autonomy who loves home and has inborn gifts for being at home and creating home. Each day she grooms herself as though she has been invited out to dinner. She becomes attached to people who come to live at Daybreak and she maintains the friendships with those who leave by remembering birthdays, visiting, and welcoming people when they come back. Thelus loves to bake cookies for someone who is ill, or to cook a meal for guests coming to Daybreak, and her welcome is genuine and warm.

When I told Joe, the Director of Daybreak, that I wanted to go to the Centre Street house, he questioned my idea of taking a time of recuperation there, because the more independent core members had requested no live-in assistants. I argued that I would not be there in the capacity of "assistant", but of "disabled". "All I can do is cry," I said, "and Ann is there as an assistant, so I have no need or desire to take responsibility for anything." Joe then said he was open to the idea, but he wanted the people who lived there to make the final decision about welcoming an assistant to live in their home. He suggested that I go to the core members and make my request to live upstairs with Peggy and Annie for a month, using the tiny spare room as my bedroom.

I went to their house meeting on Monday night when all were present with Ann, their assistant, and I tried to explain that I was not doing very well, that I felt tired and overwhelmed, and that I needed some time and space to regain my energies. With tears streaming down my face, I said that I felt I could not work for the moment, that I was prone to breaking into tears, and that I would not be a very good companion or host for guests during the time I would spend with them. I said that I thought their home would be a good place for me because we all knew each other well and I felt safe to be with them on the weekends and in the evenings. Also, because they were all out during the day, I would have lots of free space and time to be alone to rest and deal with all that I was experiencing. Then I asked if they could welcome me for a month if I promised not to come in the role of assistant.

Without hesitation they answered. "Of course you can come!" said Peggy. "Yes, it will be great to have you, " David added, and "You are welcome to our home" said Thelus, followed by, "I think you'll love it here. It's a great house!" from Peter. They saw my tears, but they were not scandalized and they were genuinely happy to welcome me!

The next day they had the room painted for me, and when I moved in, two days later, they had a huge welcome sign opposite the door as I came in the house, plus, a bouquet of flowers and a welcome card in my new room. Ever so concerned, each one took me aside in the next few days to explain one or other aspect of life in their home; David began, "You know that we take turns to do the shopping on Monday night. You don't have to take a turn unless you want to, but if you want something at the store, just put it on the list and we will get it for you." Thelus, concerned for me, announced, "We take turns cooking, but you don't have to cook unless you want to. Cooking might be good for you if you like it, so just tell us what you want to do. We cook anyway, so it is no problem for us, one way or the other." Peter told me, "I'm going to the cleaners on Friday, so if you need anything cleaned, I'll take it for you and pick it up. You might not feel like going!"

At the beginning I felt very incapable, not wanting to say much, to listen much, or to do anything! Often I would sit at the dinner table with tears streaming down my face, unable to carry on a conversation. Peggy never blinked and Annie patted me on the arm and said, "It's OK, Big Susie, You're going to be alright, Big Susie. Isn't that right, Daisy?" (her nickname for Peggy). This was so simple and so important, because they made me feel like I had no need to be other than I was, no need to try to cover my anguish, no need to disappear and let them be happy without me there. They were OK with me being in pain. Amazing!

When Peter stopped at the Dairy Queen he did not forget to bring me a treat. Thelus baked cookies downstairs, brought a plate up, put the kettle on, and called us together for tea, asking me about my day and encouraging me in the best way she could. David called up the stairs every day when he got home from work to see what kind of a day I'd had and how I was. Almost every day when I finished telling him, he called back up the stairs, "I'm so glad you are living here with us!" I could not understand how he could say that, because I felt like such an unproductive, unsupportive member of the household! It was like balm for my aching spirit.

After I went to my room early one night, I was aware that Peggy, who had been watching sports on TV right outside my door, had turned off the TV and left. I went and found her in her bedroom, lying on her bed listening to the radio. When I asked why she had left, she said that it was noisy for me and that she didn't mind listening on her radio.

For six weeks I was covered with kindness and gentleness from each one of the people at Centre Street. Having space and time was critical for me, but the safe, caring environment provided by the people was a major factor in my healing. It was so good, that when I went back to work I stayed in the home and lived with them for a whole year.

During that year we had to welcome someone into the home for four months, so we decided that Annie and I would share a bedroom. I wasn't excited to share a room with Annie, especially because I am so used to my own space and I love to go to my room after a long day. Annie proved to be an incredible room-mate though, thoughtful and considerate in the extreme. If I came in late, she had turned my bed down and gone to bed with the light on! If I left my clothes on the bed to take a shower, Annie had put them away before I got back! When I complained that I didn't have enough room for my books, she emptied the top drawer of her dresser to accommodate me! These four months, sitting on our beds talking after work, or teasing each other as we got into bed, were pure gift for me.

In the early years when I felt well and fruitful and able to welcome and support these people in their lives at Daybreak, I had no intuition that I would ever need them. It was easy for me to feel good about myself when I was in control and when I was the one who was supportive and giving. But when I lost my ability to perform, when the tables were turned and I was "grounded," thinking that I had no value apart from my work, the people of Centre Street were there, teaching me by their acceptance and their love that I was important to them as a person and not simply as a worker! They valued me when I felt I had no value in my own eyes, and they helped me to gain a new perspective on God's unconditional love.

God's unconditional love is the foundation of a family or a community. Without God, the Author of Love, we are doomed, because family, community, and human relationships are so impossible. Growth and healing become possible when, recognizing that we are children loved by God, we take each other by the hand and we learn, through trust and broken trust, joy and pain, to walk together. It is a marvelous journey.

The stories in this book are about particular L'Arche members who have been walking together now for quite a long time. Each living member, with the exception of Rosie, has listened to his or her particular chapter and has accepted that his or her story be told herein. Each one is hopeful that you, the reader, will be inspired and energized by their experience and by their growth.

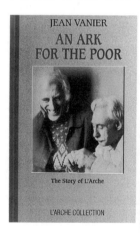